Historical Research in Music Education

A Bibliography

Second Edition

by

George N. Heller

The University of Kansas
Department of Art and Music Education and Music Therapy
311 Bailey Hall
Lawrence, Kansas 66045-2344
1992

© Department of Art and Music Education and Music Therapy
The University of Kansas, 1992

ISBN 1-879818-05-1

CONTENTS

Chapter

  I. BIOGRAPHIES 1

 II. GEOGRAPHICAL STUDIES 46

    Eastern Division 46
    North Central Division 52
    Northwestern Division 58
    Southern Division 59
    Southwestern Division 66
    Western Division 74
    Canada 76
    Central and South America 77
    Europe 78
    Africa 80
    Asia 81
    Australia and the Pacific Islands 83

III. OTHER 84

    Books 84
    Book Chapters, Periodicals, Yearbooks, and Proceedings 87
    Reviews 102
    Dissertations 107
    Theses 119

I. BIOGRAPHIES

Berry, Lemuel, Jr. *Biographical Dictionary of Black Musicians and Music Educators.* Guthrie, OK: Educational Book Publishers, 1978.

Gary, Charles L. *Vignettes of Music Education History.* Washington, DC: Music Educators National Conference, 1964.

Floyd, Samuel A., and Marsha J. Reisser. *Black Music Biography: An Annotated Bibliography.* White Plains, NY: Kraus International Publications, 1987.

Goodman, A. Harold. *Music Education Perspectives and Perceptions: Including Thirty-Seven Outstanding Music Educators.* Dubuque, IA: Kendall-Hunt Publishing Company, 1982.

Graber, Stephanie B. "A Rating Index for Use in Evaluating Music Education Leaders as Subjects of Biographical Study." Ph.D. diss., The University of Utah, 1983.

Simpson, Kenneth, ed. *Some Great Music Educators: A Collection of Essays.* Borough, Kent, England: Novello and Company, Limited, 1976.

Young, Pauline. "Significant Contributions by New England Music Educators, 1875-1940." Master's thesis, Boston University, 1951.

Adgate, Andrew (1762-1793)

Cummings, Harmon D. "Andrew Adgate: Philadelphia Psalmodist and Music Educator." Ph.D. diss., Eastman School of Music, The University of Rochester, 1975.

The New Grove Dictionary of American Music, 1986 ed. S. v. "Adgate, Andrew," by Richard Crawford.

Aiken, Charles (1818-1892)

Gary, Charles L. "Charles Aiken (1818-1892): Pioneer Apostle of Quality Music." *The Bulletin of Historical Research in Music Education* 7 (January 1986): 1-11.

Aikin, Jesse B.

Hammond, Paul G. "A Study of *The Christian Minstrel* (1846), by Jesse B. Aikin." Master's thesis, Southern Baptist Theological Seminary, 1969.

The New Grove Dictionary of American Music, 1986 ed. S.v. "Aikin, Jesse B(owman)," by Paul Hammond.

Applebaum, Samuel

Smith, G. Jean. "Pioneers in String Education: The Genius of Samuel Applebaum." *The Instrumentalist* 41 (September 1986): 30-36.

Bachman, Harold B.

Tipps, A. Wayne. "Harold B. Bachman, American Bandmaster: His Contributions and Influence." Ph.D. diss., The University of Michigan, 1974.

Bacon, Denise

Tacka, Philip A. "Denise Bacon, Musician and Educator: Contributions to the Adaptation of the Kodály Concept in the United States." D.M.A. diss., The Catholic University of America, 1982.

Bailey, John E.

"Some Veteran Supervisors: Brief Sketches of W. A. Hogdon, B. Jepson, M. Z. Tinker, J. E. Bailey, and H. M. Butler." *School Music Monthly* 4 (May 1903): 9-16.

Baldwin, Lillian

Massman, Richard L. "Lillian Baldwin and the Cleveland Plan for Educational Concerts." Ph.D. diss., The University of Michigan, 1972.

Baldwin, Ralph L. (1872-1943)

Flaherty, Avellina. "Ralph Lyman Baldwin (1872-1943): Musician and Educator." Master's thesis, The Catholic University of America, 1960.

Barnes, Edwin N. C. (1877-1952)

Elward, Thomas J. "Edwin Ninyon Chaloner Barnes: American School Musician." *The Bulletin of Historical Research in Music Education* 5 (January 1984): 1-19.

Bartlett, David Ely (1805-1879)

Darrow, Alice-Ann, and George N. Heller. "Early Advocates of Music Education for the Hearing Impaired: William Wolcott Turner and David Ely Bartlett." *Journal of Research in Music Education* 33 (Winter 1985): 269-279.

Baxter, James (1819-1897)

Swift, Frederic Fay. *James Baxter: An American Pioneer Music Educator*. Oneonta, NY: Swift-Dorr Publications, 1971.

Beach, Frank A. (1871-1935)

Kastendieck, Mary Kay. "Frank Ambrose Beach: His Life and Career in the Music Educators National Conference." Master's thesis, The University of Kansas, 1984.

The New Grove Dictionary of American Music, 1986 ed. S.v. "Beach, Frank A.," by George N. Heller.

Beattie, John W. (1885-1962)

Curtis, Louis Woodson. "The Versatile John Beattie." *Music Educators Journal* 43 (November-December 1956): 22-26.

Edwards, Larry W. "John Walter Beattie, 1885-1962: Pragmatic Music Educator." Ph.D. diss., The University of Michigan, 1971.

_____. "John Walter Beattie, 1885-1962: Pragmatic Music Educator." *The Bulletin of Historical Research in Music Education* 6 (July 1985): 45-79.

Behrend, Jeanne

Hostetter, Elizabeth A. "Jeanne Behrend: Pioneer Performer of American Music, Pianist, Teacher, Musicologist, and Composer." D.M.A. diss., Arizona State University, 1990.

Belcher, Supply (1752-1836)

The New Grove Dictionary of American Music, 1986 ed. S.v. "Belcher, Supply," by Richard Crawford.

Owen, Earl M. "The Life and Music of Supply Belcher (1752-1836), 'Handel of Maine'." D.M.A. diss., Southern Baptist Theological Seminary, 1969.

Bernstein, Leonard (1918-1990)

The New Grove Dictionary of American Music, 1986 ed. S.v. "Bernstein, Leonard," by Joan Peyser.

Rozen, Brian D. "Leonard Bernstein's Educational Legacy." *Music Educators Journal* 78 (September 1991): 43-46.

Billings, William (1746-1800)

Anderson, Gillian B. Review of *The Complete Works of William Billings*, Vol. 3. In *American Music* 7 (Summer 1989): 214-216.

Cooke, Nym. "William Billings in the District of Maine, 1780." *American Music* 9 (Fall 1991): 243-259.

Daniels, Rose Dwiggins. "William Billings: Teacher, Innovator, Patriot." *Music Educators Journal* 74 (May 1988): 22-25.

The New Grove Dictionary of American Music, 1986 ed. S.v. "Billings, William," by Karl Kroeger.

Binkowski, Bernhard (b. 1912)

Ehrenforth, Karl Heinrich. "Personalities in World Music Education No. 11—Bernhard Binkowski." *International Journal of Music Education* 16 (1990): 35-39.

Birchard, Clarence C. (1867-1946)

Jansky, Nelson M. "On the Top Floor of the Old Pope Bicycle Building." *Music Educators Journal* 60 (September 1973): 50-54, 91-94.

Birge, Edward Bailey (1868-1952)

Beattie, John W. "Appreciation of a Colleague." *Music Educators Journal* 25 (September 1938): 16.

Earhart, Will. "A Tribute to a Colleague." *Music Educators Journal* 30 (May 1944): 13, 59.

The New Grove Dictionary of American Music, 1986 ed. S.v. "Birge, Edward Bailey," by George N. Heller.

Schwartz, Charles F. "Edward Bailey Birge: His Life and Contributions to Music Education." Ph.D. diss., Indiana University, 1966.

Bivins, Alice (1888-1937)

McKinney, Jane G. "Developmental Pursuits of Excellence in North Carolina Music Education Shared by Alice Bivins, Grace VanDyke More, and Birdie Holloway During Their Careers at the University of North Carolina at Greensboro (1917-1965)." Ed.D. diss., University of North Carolina at Greensboro, 1989.

Blackman, Orlando

Devick, Royce D. "Orlando Blackman: A Study of His Contribution to Music Education in the Chicago Public Schools. (1863-1899)." Ph.D. diss., The University of Iowa, 1972.

Lawrence, William M. "A Sketch of the Late Orlando Blackman." *School Music Monthly* 1 (April 1900): 1-3.

Bolton, Thaddeus (1865-1948)

Humphreys, Jere T. "Thaddeus Bolton and the First Dissertation in Music Education." *Journal of Research in Music Education* 38 (Summer 1990): 138-148.

Bornoff, George

Smith, G. Jean. "Pioneers in String Education: The Controversial George Bornoff." *The Instrumentalist* 40 (May 1986): 14-17.

Boulanger, Nadia (1887-1979)

Brown, Bruce A. "*Leçon de Musique avec* Nadia Boulanger." *Music Educators Journal* 69 (September 1982): 49-51.

The New Grove Dictionary of American Music, 1986 ed. S.v. "Boulanger, Nadia," by Vivian Perlis.

The New Oxford Companion to Music, 1983 ed. S.v. "Boulanger, Nadia," by Paul Griffiths.

Wilde, David. "An International Music Educator: Nadia Boulanger (1877-1979)." *The International Journal of Music Education* 2 (November 1983): 36-42.

Bowen, George Oscar (1873-1957)

Spurgeon, Alan L. "George Oscar Bowen: His Career and Contributions to Music Education." Ph.D. diss., University of Oklahoma, 1990.

Bradbury, William B. (1816-1868)

The New Grove Dictionary of American Music, 1986 ed. S.v. "Bradbury, William Batchelder," by Alan B. Wingard.

Wingard, Alan B. "The Life and Works of William Batchelder Bradbury, 1816-1868." D.M.A. diss., Southern Baptist Theological Seminary, 1973.

Broudy, Harry

Dibianco, Douglas R. "Harry Broudy, Music, and the Humanities." Ph.D. diss., University of Illinois, 1975.

Brown, Elaine

Ewing, James D. "Elaine Brown and Singing City: The Choral Art as a Communicative Social Force." Ph.D. diss., University of Miami, 1976.

Brown, Francis Henry (1818-1891)

Coolidge, Arlan R. "Francis Henry Brown, 1818-1891, American Teacher and Composer." *Journal of Research in Music Education* 9 (Spring 1961): 10-26.

Bryan, Charles Faulkner (1911-1955)

King, Charles D. "Charles Faulkner Bryan: Tennessee Music Educator and Musician." Master's thesis, University of Tennessee, 1965.

Livingston, Carolyn H. "Charles Faulkner Bryan: A Biography." Ph.D. diss., University of Florida, 1986.

_____. "Charles Faulkner Bryan and American Folk Music." *The Bulletin of Historical Research in Music Education* 11 (July 1990): 76-92.

Burney, Charles (1726-1814)

Casella, Lorraine A. "Charles Burney the Pedagogue: A Critical Evaluation of the Great Historian as Music Educator." D.M.A. diss., The Catholic University of America, 1979.

Kassler, Jamie Croy. "Burney's *Sketch of a Plan for a Public Music-School*." *Musical Quarterly* 58 (April 1972): 210-234.

Burrows, Raymond (b. 1905)

Wagner, Edyth E. "Raymond Burrows and His Contributions to Music Education." D.M.A. diss., University of Southern California, 1968.

Busch, Carl (1862-1943)

Lowe, Donald R. "Carl Busch: Danish-American Music Educator." *Journal of Research in Music Education* 31 (Summer 1983): 85-92.

_____. "Sir Carl Busch: His Life and Work as a Teacher, Conductor, and Composer." D.M.A. diss., University of Missouri, Kansas City, 1972.

Butler, Henry M.

"Some Veteran Supervisors: Brief Sketches of W. A. Hogdon, B. Jepson, M. Z. Tinker, J. E. Bailey, and H. M. Butler." *School Music Monthly* 4 (May 1903): 9-16.

Buttelman, Clifford V. (1886-1970)

Runyon, Daniel. "A Buttelman Portrait." *Music Educators Journal* 67 (March 1981): 45-47.

Carney, Gerald M. (1904-1991)

Gish, Glenn R. "Gerald McKinley Carney: Midwestern Music Educator." Master's thesis, The University of Kansas, 1988.

Chapin Family

Hamm, Charles. "The Chapins and Sacred Musc in the Southand West." *Journal of Research in Music Education* 9 (Fall 1960): 91-98.

The New Grove Dictionary of American Music, 1986 ed. S.v. "Chapin," by James W. Scholten.

Scholten, James W. "Amzi Chapin: Frontier Singing Master and Folk Hymn Composer." *Journal of Research in Music Education* 23 (Summer 1975): 109-119.

_____. "The Chapins: A Study of Men and Sacred Music West of the Alleghenies, 1795-1842." Ed.D. diss., The University of Michigan, 1972.

_____. "Lucius Chapin: A New England Singing Master on the Frontier." *Contributions to Music Education* 4 (1976): 64.

Choate, Robert A. (1930-1975)

"In Memoriam: Robert A. Choate." *Music Educators Journal* 61 (March 1975): 27, 105-107.

Christiansen Family

Johnson, Albert R. "The Christiansen Choral Tradition: F. Melius Christiansen, Olaf C. Christiansen, and Paul J. Christiansen." Ph.D. diss., The University of Iowa, 1973.

The New Grove Dictionary of American Music, 1986 ed. S.v. "Christiansen, F. Melius," by Carol J. Oja.

Clapp, Philip Greeley

Holcomb, Dorothy Regina. "Philip Greeley Clapp: His Contribution to the Music of America." Ph.D. diss., The University of Iowa, 1972.

The New Grove Dictionary of American Music, 1986 ed. S.v. "Clapp, Philip Greeley," by Dorothy Regina Holcomb.

Clark, Frances Elliott (1860-1958)

Bingham, Joanne L. "A Biography of Frances Elliott Clark and Her Place in the Development of the Music Educators National Conference." Master's thesis, Peabody Conservatory of Music, 1956.

Birge, Edward Bailey. "Frances Elliott Clark: Supervisor Sketches." *Musician* 37 (June 1932): 9-10.

"Clark Centennial Memorial Tributes." *Music Educators Journal* 46 (April-May 1960): 78-79.

Cooke, James Francis, L. V. Hollweck, Marie Morrisey Keith, and Hazel G. Kinscella. "Frances Elliott Clark." *Music Educators Journal* 46 (April-May 1960): 20-24.

"Frances Elliott Clark: Eighty-Fifth Birthday." *Etude* 63 (July 1945): 361.

"Frances Elliott Clark, Ex-RCA Aide." [Obituary] *The New York Times*, 14 June 1958, p. 21.

Kinscella, Hazel G. "Mother of the Conference: A Tribute to Frances Elliott Clark." *Music Educators Journal* 42 (April-May 1956): 28-29.

The New Grove Dictionary of American Music, 1986 ed. S.v. "Clark, Frances Elliott," by George N. Heller.

Stoddard, Eugene M. "Frances Elliott Clark: Her Life and Contributions to Music Education." Ph.D. diss., Brigham Young University, 1968.

Clarke, Herbert L. (1867-1945)

Madeja, James Thomas, "The Life and Work of Herbert L. Clarke (1867-1945)." Ed.D. diss., University of Illinois, 1988.

Cogswell, Hamlin E.

Echard, Shirley Jean. "Hamlin E. Cogswell: His Life and Contributions to Music Education." D.M.A. diss., The Catholic University of America, 1973.

Cole, Samuel Winkley

Baker, James E. "Samuel Winkley Cole: New England Music Educator." D.M.A. diss., The Catholic University of America, 1975.

Coleman, Satis Naronna Barton (1878-1961)

Biographical Dictionary of American Educators, 1978 ed. S.v. "Colemen, Satis Narrona Barton," by John F. Ohles.

Southcott, Jane. "A Music Education Pioneer—Dr. Satis Naronna Barton Coleman." *British Journal of Music Education* 7 (July 1990): 123-132.

Conn, C. G. (1844-1931)

Krivin, Martin. "C. G. Conn: His Legacy and Legend." *Journal of Band Research* 1 (Winter 1965): 11-18.

The New Grove Dictionary of American Music, 1986 ed. S.v. "Conn," by Carolyn Bryant.

Corley, John

Ayoob, Kenneth P. "John Corley and the Massachusetts Institute of Technology Concert Band." *The Bulletin of Historical Research in Music Education* 13 (January 1992): 8-18.

Crane, Julia Ettie (1855-1923)

Claudson, William D. "The Philosophy of Julia E. Crane and the Origin of Music Teacher Training." *Journal of Research in Music Education* 17 (Winter 1969): 399-404.

The New Grove Dictionary of American Music, 1986 ed. S.v. "Crane, Julia E.," by Margaret William McCarthy.

Curtis, Louis W.

Hammer, Eleanor R. "Louis Woodson Curtis: Music Educator." Master's thesis, University of California at Los Angeles, 1961.

Curwen, John (1816-1880)

The New Oxford Companion to Music, 1983 ed. S.v. "Curwen," by J. N. Thomson.

Zinar, Ruth. "John Curwen: Teaching the Tonic Sol-Fa Method, 1816-1880." *Music Educators Journal* 70 (October 1983): 46-47.

Damrosch, Walter J. (1862-1950)

Goodell, Sr. M. Elaine. "Walter Damrosch and His Contribution to Music Education." D.M.A. diss., The Catholic University of America, 1973.

Martin, George W. *The Damrosch Dynasty: America's First Family of Music*. Boston: Houghton Mifflin Company, 1983.

The New Grove Dictionary of American Music, 1986 ed. S.v. "Damrosch, Family of Musicians," by H. E. Krehbiel, Richard Aldrich, H. C. Colles, and R. Allen Lott.

Perryman, William R. "Walter Damrosch: An Educational Force in American Music." Ph.D. diss., Indiana University, 1972.

Dann Hollis (1861-1939)

DeJarnette, Reven S. "Hollis Dann: His Life and Contribution to Music Education." Master's thesis, New York University, 1939.

The New Grove Dictionary of Americcan Music, 1986 ed. S.v. "Dann, Hollis Ellsworth," by William McClellan.

Davies, Peter Maxwell (b. 1934

The New Oxford Companion to Music, 1983 ed. S.v. Davies, Peter Maxwell," by Paul Griffith.

Schlotel, Brian. "Personalities in World Music Education No. 12—Peter Maxwell Davies." *International Journal of Music Education* 17 (1991): 43-47.

Davis, Katherine K

Boughton, Harrison C. "Katherine K. Davis: Life and Work." D.M.A. diss., University of Missouri, Kansas City, 1974.

Davison, Archibald T. (1883-1961)

The New Grove Dictionary of American Music, 1986 ed. S.v. "Davison, A. T.," by Jon Newsom.

Sanford, Gordon T. Review of "Archibald Thompson Davison: Harvard Musician and Scholar" (Ph.D. diss., The University of Michigan, 1979), by David G. Tovey. *Bulletin of the Council for Research in Music Education* 70 (Spring 1982): 45-47.

Tovey, David G. "Archibald Thompson Davison: Harvard Musician and Scholar." Ph.D. diss., The University of Michigan, 1979.

Davisson, Ananias (1780-1857)

Harley, Rachel A. B. "Ananias Davisson: Southern Tune-Book Compiler (1780-1857)." Ph.D. diss., The University of Michigan, 1972.

Music, David W. "Ananias Davisson, Robert Boyd, Reubin Monday, John Martin, and Archibald Rhea in East Tennessee, 1816-26." *American Music* 1 (Fall 1983): 72-84.

The New Grove Dictionary of American Music, 1986. ed S.v. "Davisson, Ananias," by Harry Eskew.

Dawson, William Levi (1899-1990)

"In Memoriam: William Levi Dawson (1899-1990)." *Choral Journal* 31 (August 1990): 32-33.

Johnson, David L. "The Contributions of William L. Dawson to the School of Music at Tuskegee Institute and to Choral Music." Ed.D. diss., University of Illinois, 1987.

Malone, Mark Hugh. "William Dawson and the Tuskegee Choir." *Choral Journal* 30 (March 1990): 17-23.

_____. "William Levi Dawson: American Music Educator." Ph.D. diss., The Florida State University, 1981.

The New Grove Dictionary of Music, 1986 ed. S. v. "Dawson, William Levi," by Eileen Southern.

Dewey, John (1859-1952)

Koob, Joseph E. "John Dewey: Music and Experience." *Music Educators Journal* 70 (January 1984): 30-32.

Zinar, Ruth. "John Dewey: Music and Progressive Education." *Music Educators Journal* 70 (January 1984): 33-34.

Diemer, Emma Lou (b. 1927)

Brown, Cynthia A. "Emma Lou Diemer: Composer, Performer, Educator, Church Musician." D.M.A. dissertation, The Southern Baptist Theological Seminary, 1985.

The New Grove Dictionary of American Music, 1986 ed. S.v. "Diemer, Emma Lou," by Sally Merrill.

Doolin, Howard

Lanier, Brian N. "Howard Doolin: His Professional Life and Contributions to Music Education." Ph.D. diss., The Florida State University, 1986.

Doyle, Price (1896-1967)

Reichmuth, Roger E. "Price Doyle, 1896-1967: His Life and Work in Music Education." Ed.D. diss., University of Illinois, 1977.

Dykema, Peter W. (1873-1951)

Beattie, John W. "The Unknown Peter Dykema." *Music Educators Journal* 37 (June-July 1951): 11.

Birge, Edward Bailey. "Supervisor Sketches." *The Musician* 37 (May 1932): 21-22.

"Dr. Peter Dykema, Educator in Music." [Obituary] *The New York Times*, 15 May, 1951, 31.

Eisenkramer, Henry E. "Peter William Dykema: His Life and Contribution to Music Education." Ed.D. diss., Teachers College, Columbia University, 1963.

Griesman, Robert J. "Early Developments Leading to Peter Dykema's Contribution to American Music Education." Master's thesis, University of Southern California, 1953.

"The Journal's First Editor." *Music Educators Journal* 37 (June-July 1951): 12.

The New Grove Dictionary of American Music, 1986 ed. S.v. "Dykema, Peter W.," by George N. Heller.

"Obituary." *Recreation* 45 (September 1951): 220.

Earhart, Will (1871-1960)

Albaugh, David H. "Will Earhart: Music Educator." Master's thesis, The University of Michigan, 1960.

Beattie, John W. "Prophet with Honor." *Music Educators Journal* 41 (February-March 1955): 21-23.

Birge, Edward Bailey. "Our Own Will Earhart." *Music Educators Journal* 27 (September-October 1940): 15.

Earhart, Will. *A Steadfast Philosophy*. Edited with and Introduction by Clifford V. Buttelman. Washington, DC: Music Educators National Conference, 1962.

McKerman, Felix E. "Will Earhart, His Life and Contributions to Music Education." Ed.D. diss., University of Southern California, 1956.

The New Grove Dictionary of American Music, 1986 ed. S.v. "Earhart, Will," by Paula Morgan and George N. Heller.

Eaton, John (1829-)

Bergee, Martin J. "Ringing the Changes: General John Eaton and the 1886 Public School Music Survey." *Journal of Research in Music Education* 35 (Summer 1987): 103-116.

Eitz, Carl (1848-1924)

Jones, Arnold. "The Tone-Word System of Carl Eitz." *Journal of Research in Music Education* 14 (Summer 1966): 84-98.

Falcone, Leonard

Welch, Myron D. "The Life and Work of Leonard Falcone with Emphasis on His Years as Director of Bands at Michigan State University, 1927 to 1967." Ed.D. diss., University of Illinois, 1973.

Farnsworth, Charles H.(1859-1947)

Birge, Edward Bailey. "Supervisor Sketches." *The Musician* 38 (May 1933): 8-9.

Lee, William R. "Education Through Music: The Life and Work of Charles Hubert Farnsworth (1859-1947)." Ph.D. diss., University of Kentucky, 1982.

_____. "The Snedden-Farnsworth Exchanges of 1917 and 1918 on the Value of Music and Art Education." *Journal of Research in Music Education* 31 (Fall 1983): 203-213.

Farwell, Arthur (1872-1952)

Davis, Evelyn H. "The Significance of Arthur Farwell as an American Music Educator." Ph.D. diss., University of Maryland, 1972.

The New Grove Dictionary of American Music, 1986 ed. S.v. "Farwell, Arthur," by Gilbert Chase and Neely Bruce.

Flagg, Marion

Delaney, Carole J. "The Contribution of Marion Flagg to Music and Education." D.M.A. diss., The University of Texas, 1974.

Franklin, Benjamin (1706-1790)

Heller, George N. "'To Sweeten Their Senses': Music, Education, and Benjamin Franklin." *Music Educators Journal* 73 (January 1987): 22-26.

The New Grove Dictionary of American Music, 1986 ed. S.v. "Franklin, Benjamin," by W. Thomas Marrocco.

Fukui, Naoaki (1877-1963)

Miayamoto, Kiyoshi, and Jocelyn Carmichael. "Japan's Naoaki Fukui and His World-Class Music School." *Music Educators Journal* 76 (December 1989): 41-45.

Fuller, O. Anderson (b. 1904)

Houser, Stephen D. "O. Anderson Fuller, the First Black Doctor of Philosophy in America, and His Development of the Music Education Curriculum at Lincoln University," Ph.D. diss., University of Missouri, Columbia, 1982.

Fullerton, Charles A. (1861-1945)

Sheckler, Lewis R. "Charles Alexander Fullerton: His Life and Contribution to Music Education." Ed.D. diss., University of Illinois, 1965.

Wolfe, Irving. "Rural School Music Missionary." *Music Educators Journal* 46 (April-May 1960): 26-28.

Gante, Pedro de (c. 1480-1572)

Heller, George N. "Fray Pedro de Gante: Pioneer American Music Educator." *Journal of Research in Music Education* 27 (Spring 1979): 20-28.

Gaston, E. Thayer (1901-1970)

Johnson, Robert E. "E. Thayer Gaston: Contributions to Music Therapy and Music Education." Ph.D. diss., The University of Michigan, 1973.

_____. "E. Thayer Gaston: Leader in Scientific Thought on Music in Therapy and Education." *Journal of Research in Music Education* 29 (Winter 1981): 279-286.

The New Grove Dictionary of American Music, 1986ed. S.v. "Gaston, E. Thayer," by George N. Heller.

Gehrkens, Karl W. (1882-1975)

Birge, Edward Bailey, "Tribute to a Colleague." *Music Educators Journal* 29 (November-December 1942): 10.

Lendrim, Frank T. "Music for Every Child: The Story of Karl Wilson Gehrkens." Ph.D. diss., The University of Michigan, 1962.

The New Grove Dictionary of American Music, 1986 ed. S.v. "Gehrkens, Karl," by George N. Heller.

Van Peursem, James E. "In Memoriam: Karl W. Gehrkens." *Music Educators Journal* 61 (May 1975): 30-31.

Gerrish, Samuel

Gates, J. Terry. "Samuel Gerrish, Publisher to the 'Regular Singing' Movement in 1720s New England." *Music Library Association Notes* 45 (September 1988): 15-22.

Giddings, Thaddeus P. (1868-1954)

Birge, Edward Bailey. "Supervisor Sketches." *The Musician* 38 (January 1933): 6-7.

Giddings, Thaddeus P. "Early Events in the Professional Life of One T. P. Giddings." *Music Supervisors Journal* 13 (February 1927): 13, 15, 67.

Kuersteiner, Karl O. "The Functional Mr. Giddings." *Music Educators Journal* 34 (September 1947): 28-29.

McDermid, Charles M. "Thaddeus P. Giddings: A Biography." Ph.D. diss., The University of Michigan, 1967.

The New Grove Dictionary of American Music, 1986 ed. S.v. "Giddings, Thaddeus P.," by George N. Heller

Gildersleeve, Glenn

Olenchak, Frank R. "Glenn Gildersleeve and His Contributions to Music Education." Ph.D. diss., The University of Michigan, 1977.

Gilmore, Patrick S. (1829-1892)

Humphreys, Jere T. "Strike Up the Band! The Legacy of Patrick S. Gilmore." *Music Educators Journal* 74 (October 1987): 22-26.

The New Grove Dictionary of American Music, 1986 ed. S.v. "Gilmore, Patrick S.," by Frank J. Cipolla.

Nicholson, Jon S. "Patrick Gilmore's Boston Peace Jubilees." Ed.D. diss., The University of Michigan, 1971.

Glenn, Mabelle (1881-1969)

Holgate, George. *The Life of Mabelle Glenn Music Educator*. West Yarmouth, MA: Rainbow Press, 1965.

_____. "Mabelle Glenn: Her Life and Contributions to Music Education." Ed.D. diss., University of Southern California, 1962.

The New Grove Dictionary of American Music, 1986 ed. S.v. "Glenn, Mabelle," by George N. Heller.

Glover, Sarah (1786-1867)

Bennett, Peggy. "Sarah Glover: A Forgotten Pioneer in Music Education." *Journal of Research in Music Education* 32 (Spring 1984): 49-65.

Goldman, Richard Franko (1910-1980)

Lester, Noel K. "Richard Franko Goldman: His Life and Works." D.M.A. diss., Peabody Conservatory of Music, 1984.

The New Grove Dictionary of American Music, 1986 ed. S.v. "Goldman, Richard Franko," by Dorothy Klotzman.

Gordon, Edgar B. (1875-1961)

Angevine, Brian C. "'Dear Pop': A Biography of Edgar B. Gordon." Ph.D. diss., The University of Kansas, 1985.

Barresi, Anthony L. "Edgar B. Gordon: A Pioneer in Music Education." *Journal of Research in Music Education* 35 (Winter 1987): 259-274.

Beattie, John W. "Edgar B. Gordon: Sociological Musician." *Music Educators Journal* 44 (November -December 1957): 31-32.

The New Grove Dictionary of American Music, 1986 ed. S.v. "Gordon, Edgar B(ernard)," by George N. Heller.

Gordon, Edwin E.

Gordon, Edwin. "Gordon on Gordon." *The Quarterly* 2 (Spring-Summer 1991): 6-9.

Gould, Glenn (1932-1982)

Angilette, Elizabeth. "Glenn Gould (1932-1982): A Study of His Contributions to a Philosophy of Music and Music Education." Ph.D. diss., New York University, 1988.

Green, Elizabeth A. H. (b. 1906)

Sanford, Gordon T. Review of "Elizabeth A. H. Green: A Biography" (Ph.D. diss., The University of Michigan, 1986) Deborah Annette Smith. In *Bulletin of the Council for Research in Music Education* 100 (Spring 1989): 66-67.

Smith, Deborah A. "Elizabeth A. H. Green: A Biography." Ph.D. diss., The University of Michigan, 1986.

Guido of Arezzo (c. 995-1050)

Miller, Samuel D. "Guido d'Arezzo: Medieval Musician and Educator." *Journal of Research in Music Education* 21 (Fall 1973): 239-245.

Hach, H. Theodore

Fisher, Robert E. "H. Theodore Hach and *The Musical Magazine*: A Historical Perspective." *Bulletin of the Council for Research in Music Education* 92 (Summer 1987): 35-46.

Hall, G. Stanley ((1842-1924)

Rideout, Roger R. "Granville Stanley Hall and Music Education: 1880-1924." Ed.D. diss., University of Illinois, 1978.

_____. "On Early Applications of Psychology in Music Education." *Journal of Research in Music Education* 30 (Fall 1982): 141-150.

Hall, Phillmore M.

Hodge, Johnny B. "A Biography of Phillmore Mallard Hall with Particular Emphasis on His Contribution to the Development of Black School Bands in North Carolina." Ph.D. diss., The American University, 1977.

Hampton, Oliver C.

Smith, Harold V. "Oliver C. Hampton and Other Shaker Teacher-Musicians of Ohio and Kentucky." D.A. diss., Ball State University, 1981.

Hanby, Benjamin Russel (1833-1867)

Gross, Jeanne B. "Benjamin Russel Hanby, Ohio Composer-Educator, 1833-1867: His Contributions to Early Music Education." Ph.D. diss., The Ohio State University, 1987.

The New Grove Dictionary of American Music, 1986 ed. S.v. "Hanby Benjamin R.," by Dale Cockrell.

Hanson, Howard (1896-1981)

"The Giant: Excerpts from the Writings of Howard Hanson." *Music Educators Journal* 68 (October 1981): 49-51.

Monroe, Robert C. "Howard Hanson: American Music Educator." Ph.D. diss., The Florida State University, 1970.

The New Grove Dictionary of American Music, 1986 ed. S.v. "Hanson, Howard," by Ruth T. Watanabe.

Harding, Albert Austin (1880-1958)

The New Grove Dictionary of American Music, 1986 ed. S.v. "Harding, Albert Austin," by Raoul Camus.

Weber, Calvin E. "Albert Austin Harding: Pioneer College Bandmaster." *Journal of Band Research* 3 (Autumn 1966): 5-12.

_____. "The Contribution of Albert Austin Harding and His Influence on the Development of School and College Bands." Ed.D. diss., University of Illinois, 1963.

Harper, James C.

Hammond, Frank M. "James Cunningham Harper and the Lenoir, North Carolina High School Band." Ed.D. diss., The University of North Carolina at Greensboro, 1973.

Harrison, Thomas

Elward, Thomas J. "Thomas Harrison's Patented Numeral Notation System." *Journal of Research in Music Education* 28 (Winter 1980): 218-224.

Harwood, Frederick

Rye, Ann B. "Frederick Harwood and Henderson State Teachers College: A History." D.M.A. diss., University of Oklahoma, 1987.

Hastings, Thomas (1784-1872)

Dooley, James E. "Thomas Hastings: American Church Musician." Ph.D. diss., Florida State University, 1963.

The New Grove Dictionary of American Music, 1986 ed. S.v. "Hastings, Thomas," by Richard Crawford.

Teal, Mary D. "Letters of Thomas Hastings." *Music Library Association Notes* 34 (December 1977): 303-318.

Hayden, Philip C. (1854-1925)

Channon, Chester N. "The Contributions of Philip Cady Hayden to Music Education in the United States." Ed.D. diss., The University of Michigan, 1959.

Hazelman, Herbert R.

Jeffreys, Harold L. "The Career of Herbert R. Hazelman: Public School Bandmaster." Ed.D. diss., University of North Carolina at Greensboro, 1988.

Secrest, Joseph D. Review of "The Career of Herbert R. Hazelman: Public School Band Master" (Ed.D. diss., The University of North Carolina at Greensboro, 1988) by Harold L. Jeffreys. *Bulletin of the Council for Research in Music Education* 107 (Winter 1991): 49-53.

Herford, Julius (1901-1981)

The New Grove Dictionary of American Music, 1986 ed. S.v. "Herford, Julius."

Hylton, John. Review of "Julius Herford: His Life, Teaching, and Influence on the Choral Art in the United States" (D.A. diss., University of Northern Colorado, 1988), by Edward E. Price. *Bulletin of the Council for Research in Music Education* 110 (Fall 1991): 83-85.

Pierce, Edward E. "Julius Herford: His Life, Teaching, and Influences on the Choral Art in the United States." D.A. diss. University of Northern Colorado, 1988.

Hindemith, Paul (1895-1963)

The New Grove Dictionary of American Music, 1986 ed. S.v. "Hindemith, Paul," by Ian Kemp and H. Wiley Hitchcock.

Vernazza, Marcelle. "Paul Hindemith—Music Educator." *The American Music Teacher* 33 (June-July 1984): 30-32.

Hindsley, Mark (b. 1905)

Croft, James E. Review of "Mark Hindsley: The Illinois Years" (Ed.D. diss., University of Illinois, 1983) by Earle S. Gregory. *Bulletin of the Council for Research in Music Education* 79 (Summer 1984): 84-90.

Gregory, Earle S. "Mark H. Hindsley: The Illinois Years." Ed.D. diss., University of Illinois, 1982.

The New Grove Dictionary of American Music, 1986 ed. S.v. "Hindsley, Mark Hubert," by Raoul Camus.

Hodgson, Hugh

McDade, Michael B. "Hugh Hodgson: The Fostering of Music in Georgia (1928-1960)." Ed.D. diss., University of Georgia, 1988.

_____. "Hugh Hodgson: The Fostering of Music in Georgia." *Georgia Music News* 51 (Fall 1990): 51-53.

Hogdon, William A.

Suehs, Hermann C. "The Legacy of William Augustus Hogdon, School Music Teacher." Master's thesis, The Catholic University of America, 1971.

"Some Veteran Supervisors: Brief Sketches of W. A. Hogdon, B. Jepson, M. Z. Tinker, J. E. Bailey, and H. M. Butler." *School Music Monthly* 4 (May 1903): 9-16.

"William A. Hogdon, St. Louis." *School Music Monthly* 7 (September 1906): 5-7.

Holloway, Birdie (b. 1899)

McKinney, Jane G. "Developmental Pursuits of Excellence in North Carolina Music Education Shared by Alice Bivins, Grace VanDyke More, and Birdie Holloway During Their Careers at the University of North Carolina at Greensboro (1917-1965)." Ed.D. diss., University of North Carolina at Greensboro, 1989.

Holt, Hosea E. (1836-1898)

Holt, Alice M. "A Sketch of the Late Hosea E. Holt." *School Music Monthly* 1 (June 1900): 1-2.

Holyoke, Samuel Adams (1762-1820)

The New Grove Dictionary of American Music, 1986 ed. S.v. "Holyoke, Samuel," by Richard Crawford.

Willhide, James L. "Samuel Holyoke, Pioneer American Music Educator." Ph.D. diss., University of Southern California, 1954.

Hopkinson, Francis (1737-1791)

Mahan, Katherine Hines. "Hopkinson and Reinagle: Patriot-Musicians of Washington's Time." *Music Educators Journal* 62 (April 1976): 40-50.

The New Grove Dictionary of American Music, 1986 ed. S.v. "Hopkinson, Francis," by Richard Crawford.

Horn, Charles Edward (1786-1849)

Montague, Richard A. "Charles Edward Horn: His Life and Works (1786-1849)." Ed.D. diss., The Florida State University, 1959.

The New Grove Dictionary of American Music, 1986 ed. S.v. "Horn, Charles Edward," by Nicolas Temperley.

Hosmer, Helen M. (1898-1989)

Bearss, Joyce. "Helen Hosmer: Potsdam's First Lady Conductor and Educator." *Choral Journal* 30 (August 1989): 15-19.

"Helen Hosmer, Renowned Music Educator, Dies at 91." *Choral Journal* 30 (March 1990): 37-38.

Lebaron, Bruce V. "Helen M. Hosmer's Philosophy of Music Education and Its Implementation." Ed.D. diss., The University of Florida, 1976.

Irons, Earl D.

Barrow, Gary W. "Colonel Earl D. Irons and the Early Development of Texas Bands." *The Journal of Band Research* 21 (Fall 1985): 9-30.

_____. "Colonel Earl D. Irons: His Role in the History of Music Education in the Southwest to 1958." Ph.D. diss., North Texas State University, 1982.

Heller, George N. Review of "Colonel Earl D. Irons: His Role in the History of Music Education in the Southwest to 1958" (Ph.D. diss., North Texas State University, 1982), by Gary Wayne Barrow. *Bulletin of the Council for Research in Music Education* 76 (Fall 1983): 65-67.

Irvin, Rev. Samuel M.

Heller, George N. "Teaching the Students in Their Own Language: The Reverend Samuel M. Irvin, Kansas Music Educator." *Kansas Music Review* 44 (December 1982): 10-11.

Ives, Charles E. (1874-1954)

Mortenson, Gary C. "Father and Son: The Education of Charles Ives." *Music Educators Journal* 73 (March 1987): 33-37.

The New Grove Dictionary of American Music, 1986 ed. S.v. "Ives, Charles (Edward)," by John Kirkpatrick and Paul C. Echols.

Wallach, Laurence D. "The New England Education of Charles Ives." Ph.D. diss., Columbia University, 1973.

Ives, Elam, Jr. (1802-1864)

John, Robert W. "Elam Ives and the Pestalozzian Philosophy of Music Education." *Journal of Research in Music Education* (Spring 1960): 45-50.

The New Grove Dictionary of American Music, 1986 ed. S.v. "Ives, Elam, Jr.," by William McClellan.

Pemberton, Carol A. "A Look at the *Juvenile Lyre* (1831): Posing a Rationale for Music in the Schools." *The Bulletin of Historical Research in Music Education* 11 (January 1990): 17-32.

Jacobi, Roger

"Summer Memories: Roger Jacobi Looks Back." *Music Performance Resources*, Spring 1990, 3-4, 11, 19, 27, 30.

Jacobs, Walter

Brandon, Stephen P. "Walter Jacobs and *Jacobs' Band Monthly*." *The Journal of Band Research* 11 (Spring 1975): 40-44.

Jepson, Benjamin (1832-1914)

Heller, George N. "Benjamin Jepson on Elementary Music: Back to Basics in '85." *Update* 3 (Spring 1985): 23-24.

Jepson, Benjamin. "Reminiscences of Early Days in School Music." *School Music* 8 (March 1908): 5-9; and (May 1908): 5-9.

_____. "Reminiscences of My Forty-Six Years of Music Supervision." *MTNA Proceedings* (1910): 20-30.

"Some Veteran Supervisors: Brief Sketches of W. A. Hogdon, B. Jepson, M. Z. Tinker, J. E. Bailey, and H. M. Butler." *School Music Monthly* 4 (May 1903): 9-16.

Jessye, Eva (b. 1895)

The New Grove Dictionary of American Music, 1986 ed. S.v. "Jessye, Eva," by Mark Tucker.

Wilson, Doris L. Jones. "Eva Jessye: Afro-American Choral Director." Ed.D. diss., Washington University, 1989.

Johnson, A. N. (1817-1892)

The New Grove Dictionary of American Music, 1986 ed. S.v. "Johnson, A. N.," by Jacklin Bolton Stopp.

Stopp, Jacklin Bolton. "A. N. Johnson: Out of Oblivion." *American Music* 3 (Summer 1985): 152-170.

Kabalevsky, Dmitry (b. 1904)

Dimentman, Boris. "Kabalevsky: Music Educator." *International Journal of Music Education* 1 (May 1983): 35-38.

Katz, Erich (1900-1973)

Primus, Constance. "Erich Katz: The Pied Piper Comes to America." *American Music Research Center Journal* 1 (1991): 1-19.

Kelley, Edgar Stillman (1857-1944)

King, Maurice R. "Edgar Stillman Kelley: American Composer, Teacher, and Author." Ph.D. diss., The Florida State University, 1970.

The New Grove Dictionary of American Music, 1986 ed. S.v. "Kelley, Edgar Stillman," by Katherine K. Preston.

Kendel, John C.

Mercer, James R. "John Clark Kendel: His View and Contributions to Music Eduction." Ph.D. diss., University of Colorado, 1972.

Klein, Maynard (1910-1990)

"In Memoriam: Maynard Klein (1910-1990)." *Choral Journal* 31 (August 1990): 32.

Kodály, Zoltán (1882-1967)

Bennett, Peggy. "From Hungary to America: The Evolution of Education Through Music." *Music Educators Journal* 74 (September 1987): 36-45.

Miller, Samuel D. "Zoltán Kodály as Musician-Educator Exemplar: A Critique." *College Music Symposium* 20 (Spring 1980): 126-135.

Stone, Margaret L. "Kodály and Orff Music Techniques: History and Present Practice." Ph.D. diss., Kent State University, 1971.

Krehbiel, Clayton H. (1920-1988)

Griffin, Philip W. "Clayton Henry Krehbiel: Musician, Educator." Ph.D. diss. The Florida State University, 1988.

Law, Andrew (1749-1821)

Crawford, Richard A. *Andrew Law: American Psalmodist*. Evanston, IL: Northwestern University Press, 1968.

_____. "Andrew Law (1749-1821): The Career of an American Musician." Ph.D. diss., The University of Michigan, 1965.

The New Grove Dictionary of American Music, 1986 ed. S.v. "Law, Andrew," by Richard Crawford.

Lawler, Vannett (1902-1972)

Izdebski, Christy. "Vanett Lawler: Her Contributions to National and International Communications in Music." *The International Journal of Music Education* 2 (November 1983): 45-48.

_____. "Vanett Lawler (1902-1972): Her Life and Contributions to Music Education." D.M.A. diss.,, The Catholic University of America, 1983.

Izdebski, Christy, and Michael L. Mark. "Vannett Lawler: International Music Education Administrator." *The Bulletin of Historical Research in Music Education* 8 (January 1987): 1-32.

Lehmann, Lotte (1888-1976)

Brown, Kathy H. "Lotte Lehmann: Artist Teacher." D.M.A. diss., University of Missouri-Kansas City, 1990.

The New Grove Dictionary of American Music, 1986 ed. S.v. "Lehmann, Lotte," by Desmond Shawe-Taylor.

Leonhard, Charles (b. 1915)

Bennett, Barbara L. "The Leonhard Connection." *Bulletin of the Council for Research in Music Education* 110 (Fall 1991): 3-20.

Kritzmire, Judith A. "The Pedagogy of Charles Leonhard: A Documentary Case Study." Ed.D. diss., University of Illinois, 1987.

The New Grove Dictionary of American Music, 1986 ed. S.v. "Leonhard, Charles," by George N. Heller.

Lesinsky, Adam P.

Hume, M. Carlyle. "Adam P. Lesinsky: A Biography." Ed.D. diss., The University of Michigan, 1971.

Lombard, Louis (1861-1927)

Lowens, Irving. "Louis Lombard's 'Our Conservatories'." *American Music* 3 (Fall 1985): 347-351.

Luther, Martin (1483-1546)

Kelley, William A. "The Relationship of the Early Lutheran Hymns to Certain Features of Martin Luther's Theories of Religious Education." Ph.D. diss., New York University, 1957.

Tarry, Joe E. "Music in the Education Philosophy of Martin Luther." *Journal of Research in Music Education* 21 (Winter 1973): 355-365.

Lutkin, Peter Christian (1858-1931)

Kennel, Pauline G. "Peter Christian Lutkin: Northwestern University's First Dean of Music." Ph.D. diss., Northwestern University, 1981.

The New Grove Dictionary of American Music, 1986 ed. S.v. "Peter Christian," by Bruce Carr.

Lyons, Howard R.

Borich, George R. "The Lives of Howard Raymond Lyons and Hubert Estel Nutt, Co-Founders of the Mid-West National Band and Orchestra Clinic." Ph.D. diss., Northwestern University, 1984.

Maddy, Joseph E. (1891-1966)

Britton, Allen P. "Point of View." *The International Journal of Music Education* 2 (November 1983): 64-66.

Browning, Norma Lee. *Joe Maddy of Interlochen*. Chicago: Henry Regnery Company, 1963.

Heller, George N. "Science, Art, and Joseph E. Maddy: Public School Music in 1938." *Update* 6 (Fall 1987): 6.

The New Grove Dictionary of American Music, 1986 ed. S.v. "Maddy, Joseph E.," by George N. Heller.

Mancini, Frank

Susca, Vito G. "Frank Mancini: His Life and Contribution to Music Education." D.M.A. diss., University of Southern California, 1967.

Mason, Daniel Gregory (1873-1953)

Klein, Mary J. "The Contribution of Daniel Gregory Mason to American Music." Ph.D. diss., The Catholic University of America, 1957.

Kushner, Leslie C. "The Prose Works of Daniel Gregory Mason: A Contribution to Music Education." Ph.D. diss., University of Florida, 1988.

Lewis, Ralph B. "The Life and Music of Daniel Gregory Mason." Ph.D. diss., University of Rochester, 1957.

The New Grove Dictionary of American Music, 1986 ed. S.v. "Mason," by Harry Eskew, W. Thomas Marrocco, Mark Jacobs, William E. Boswell, and Boris Schwarz.

Mason, Lowell (1792-1872)[1]

Barnard, Henry. "Lowell Mason." *American Journal of Education* 4 (1858): 146.

Brinckmeyer, Lynn M. Review of *Lowell Mason: A Bio-Bibliography*, by Carol A. Pemberton. *The Bulletin of Historical Research in Music Education* 10 (July 1989): 118-118.

Darrow, Alice-Ann. Review of *Lowell Mason: His Life and Work* by Carol A. Pemberton. *The Bulletin of Historical Research in Music Education* 7 (January 1986): 29-32.

Darrow, Alice-Ann, and George N. Heller. "Lowell Mason (1792-1872): Early American Music Therapist." *Journal of the International Association of Music for the Handicapped* 3 (Winter 1988): 3-17.

Dunkelberger, Gustav. "Lowell Mason and the Beginning of Music Education." Master's thesis, University of Chicago, 1944.

Heller, George N. Review of *Lowell Mason: His Life and Work*, by Carol A. Pemberton. In *Music Educators Journal* 72 (December 1985): 59-61.

Keating, Mary F. "Lowell Mason in Savannah." *The Bulletin of Historical Research in Music Education* 10 (July 1989): 73-84.

Mason, Lowell. *A Yankee Musician in Europe: The 1837 Journals of Lowell Mason* Edited with and Introduction by Michael Broyles. Ann Arbor, MI: UMI Research Press, 1990.

Pemberton, Carol A. "A Look at the *Juvenile Lyre* (1831): Posing a Rationale for Music in the Schools." *The Bulletin of Historical Research in Music Education* 11 (January 1990): 17-32.

_____. *Lowell Mason: A Bio-Bibliography*. New York: Greenwood Press, 1988.

---

[1]All items in Carol A. Pemberton, *Lowell Mason: A Bio-Bibliography* (New York: Greenwood Press, 1988) are omitted. Items published since that time and the very few items published before 1988 which Pemberton did not include are listed.

_____. "Lowell Mason and His Mission." *Music Educators Journal* 78 (January 1992): 49-52.

_____. "Instituting Music in the Boston Public School Curriculum: A Classic Example of the Diffusion of Innovation." *Knowledge in Society* 1 (Fall 1988): 69-79.

Porter, Susan L. "Lowell Mason Revisited: Sight-Singing Among Children." *The Sonneck Society Bulletin* 13 (Summer 1987): 46-47.

Pound, Gomer. "Mason's Hand in 'Mary's Lamb'." *The Bulletin of Historical Research in Music Education* 7 (January 1986): 23-27.

"Reprints from Lowell Mason's *Manual of the Boston Academy of Music*, 5th ed. (Boston, 1843)." *The Bulletin of Historical Research in Music Education* 11 (July 1990): 110-137; Part II. *The Bulletin of Historical Research in Music Education* 12 (January 1991): 50-62; Part III. *The Bulletin of Historical Research in Music Education* 12 (July 1991): 129-145; Part IV. *The Bulletin of Historical Research in Music Education* 13 (January 1992): 33-54.

Rich, Arthur L. "Lowell Mason, Music Educator." Ph.D. diss., New York University, 1940.

Scholten, James W. "Lowell Mason and His Shape-Note Tunebook in the Ohio Valley: The Sacred Harp, 1834-1850." *Contributions to Music Education* 15 (Fall 1988): 47-52.

Van Camp, Leonard. "1838: Lowell Mason Uses Music with Children to Inspire 'Habits of Order and Union'." *Choristers Guild Letters* 39 (February 1988): 150-153.

_____. "Lowell Mason: A Life to Celebrate." *Choristers Guild Letters* 39 (January 1988): 117-118.

Mason, Luther Whiting (1818-1896)

Arnett, Earl. "Rediscovery of a Unique Music Educator." *Music Educators Journal* 59 (May 1973): 60-61.

Berger, Donald P. "Isawa Shuji and Luther Whiting Mason: Pioneers of Music Education in Japan." *Music Educators Journal* 74 (October 1987): 31-36.

Hall, Bonlyn F. "The American Education of Luther Whiting Mason." *American Music* 6 (Spring 1988): 65-73.

_____. "Luther Whiting Mason's European Song Books." *Music Library Association Notes* 41 (March 1985): 482-491.

Hartley, Kenneth. "A Study of the Life and Works of Luther Whiting Mason." Ed.D. diss., The Florida State University, 1960.

Howe, Sondra Wieland. "Luther Whiting Mason: Contributions to Music Education in Nineteenth-Century America and Japan." Ph.D. diss., University of Minnesota, 1988.

_____. "'The Tempest of War': Luther Whiting Mason in the American Civil War." *The Bulletin of Historical Research in Music Education* 12 (July 1991): 100-112.

The New Grove Dictionary of American Music, 1986 ed. S.v. "Mason, Luther Whiting," by Bonlyn Hall.

Mason, William (1829-1908)

Graber, Kenneth G. "The Life and Works of William Mason (1829-1908)." Ph.D. diss., The University of Iowa, 1976.

_____. *William Mason (1829-1908): An Annotated Bibliography and Catalog of Works*. Warren, MI: Harmonie Park Press.

The New Grove Dictionary of American Music, 1986 ed. S.v. "Mason," by Harry Eskew, W. Thomas Marrocco, Mark Jacobs, William E. Boswell, and Boris Schwarz.

Mattern, David E.

Hanson, Merle J. "David Earl Mattern: A Biography." Ph.D. diss., The University of Michigan, 1974.

McBurney, Samuel (1847-1909)

Stevens, Robin S. "Samuel McBurney: Australian Advocate of Tonic Sol-Fa." *Journal of Research in Music Education* 34 (Summer 1986): 77-87.

McConathy, Osbourne (1875-1947)

Buttelman, Clifford V. "Osbourne McConathy." *Music Educators Journal* 33 (April 1947): 15.

The New Grove Dictionary of American Music, 1986 ed. S.v. "McConathy, Osbourne," by George N. Heller.

Platt, Melvin C. "Osbourne McConathy: American Music Educator." Ph.D. diss., The University of Michigan, 1971.

_____. "Osbourne McConathy: American Music Educator." *Journal of Research in Music Education* 21 (Summer 1973): 169-175.

Medley, John

Cooper, Timothy G. "John Medley: Canadian Choral Pioneer." *Choral Journal* 31 (September 1990): 35-36.

Miessner, W. Otto (1880-1967)

Miller, Samuel D. "W. Otto Miessner and His Contributions to Music in American Schools." Ph.D. diss., The University of Michigan, 1962.

_____. "Visionary of What Might Be: The Story of W. Otto Miessner." *The Bulletin of Historical Research in Music Education* 2 (July 1981): 21-34.

The New Grove Dictionary of American Music, 1986 ed. S.v. "Miessner, W. Otto," by George N. Heller.

Milam, Lena (1884-1984)

Babil, Louis R. "Lena Milam, 1884-1984: Music Educator and Pioneer in the Development of Community Music in Beaumont, Texas." Ph.D. diss., Louisiana State University, 1987.

Montessori, Maria (1870-1952)

Faulmann, Jo. "Montessori and Music in Early Childhood." *Music Educators Journal* 66 (May 1980): 41-43.

Moore, Undine Smith

Harris, Carl. "Conversations with Undine Smith Moore: Composer and Master Teacher." *The Black Perspective in Music* 13 (Spring 1985): 79-90.

The New Grove Dictionary of American Music, 1986 ed. S.v. "Moore, Undine Smith," by Doris Evans McGinty.

More, Grace Van Dyke (1884-1960)

McKinney, Jane G. "Developmental Pursuits of Excellence in North Carolina Music Education Shared by Alice Bivins, Grace VanDyke More, and Birdie Holloway During Their Careers at the University of North Carolina at Greensboro (1917-1965)." Ed.D. diss., University of North Carolina at Greensboro, 1989.

Mozart, Wolfgang Amadeus (1756-1791)

Mann, Alfred, and Mario R. Mercado. "Mozart as a Teacher." *American Music Teacher* 41 (October-November 1991): 18-21, 45-47.

Murphy, Howard

Olsen, Richard N. "Howard A. Murphy, Theorist and Teacher: His Influence on the Teaching of Basic Music Theory in American Colleges and Universities from 1940 to 1973." Ed.D. diss., University of Illinois, 1973.

Mursell, James L. (1893-1963)

Gehrkens, Karl W. "Tribute to James Mursell." *Music Educators Journal* 50 (September-October 1963): 16, 18.

Heller, George N. "Carl Emil Seashore and James Lockhart Mursell: The Famous Controversy—Did It Ever Exist?" *Update* 4 (Spring 1986): 13-14.

Metz, Donald E. "A Critical Analysis of the Thought of James L. Mursell in Music Education." Ph.D. diss., Case Western Reserve University, 1968.

_____. "Inconsistencies in the Writings of James L. Mursell." *Bulletin of the Council for Research in Music Education Bulletin* 23 (Winter 1971): 6-11.

The New Grove Dictionary of American Music, 1986 ed. S.v. "Mursell, James L.," by George N. Heller.

O'Keefe, Vincent C. "James Lockhart Mursell, His Life and Contributions to Music Education."" Ed.D. diss., Teachers College, Columbia University, 1970.

Simutis, Leonard J. "James L. Mursell: An Annotated Bibliography." *Journal of Research in Music Education* 16 (Fall 1968): 254-266.

Wilson, Harry Robert. "James L. Mursell." *Music Educators Journal* 49 (April-May 1963): 116-117.

Nutt, Hubert E.

Borich, George R. "The Lives of Howard Raymond Lyons and Hubert Estel Nutt, Co-Founders of the Mid-West National Band and Orchestra Clinic." Ph.D. diss., Northwestern University, 1984.

Oliver, Henry Kemble (1800-1885)

Knight, Harold A. "The Life and Musical Activities of Henry Kemble Oliver (1800-1885)." Ph.D. diss., University of Iowa, 1988.

Orff, Carl (b. 1895)

Stone, Margaret L. "Kodály and Orff Music Techniques: History and Present Practice." Ph.D. diss., Kent State University, 1971.

Velásquez, Vivian. "Tuned Idiophones in the Music Education of Children: The History of Orff Instruments." *The Bulletin of Historical Research in Music Education* 11 (July 1990): 93-109.

Padilla, Juan de (c. 1500-1542)

Heller, George N. "Fray Juan de Padilla: The First Euro American Music Educator." *Kansas Music Review* 44 (October-November 1982): 6.

The New Grove Dictionary of American Music, 1986 ed. S.v. "Padilla, Juan de," by George N. Heller.

Paine, John Knowles (1839-1906)

Huxford, John. "John Knowles Paine: His Life and Works." Ph.D. diss., The Florida State University, 1968.

The New Grove Dictionary of American Music, 1986 ed. S.v. "Paine, John Knowles," by Kenneth C. Roberts, Jr. and John C. Schmidt.

Parker, Alice (b. 1925)

Latta, John A. "Alice Parker: Composer, Arranger, and Teacher." Ed.D. diss., University of Illinois, 1986.

Mussulman, Joseph A. "Alice Parker: Riding a Surfboard." *Music Educators Journal* 66 (March 1980): 42-45, 90-91.

Parker, Horatio (1863-1919)

Kearns, William K. *Horatio Parker, 1863-1919: His Life, Music, and Ideas*. Metuchen, NJ: The Scarecrow Press, Inc., 1990.

_____. "Horatio Parker, 1863-1919: A Study of His Life and Music." Ph.D. diss., University of Illinois, 1965.

The New Grove Dictionary of American Music, 1986 ed. S.v. "Parker, Horatio (William)," by William Kearns.

Perkins Family

Comstock, Raymond D. "Contributions of the Orson Perkins Family to Nineteenth-Century American Music Education." Ph.D. diss., The University of Iowa, 1970.

The New Grove Dictionary of American Music, 1986 ed. S.v. "Perkins, Henry S.," by Ramond D. Comstock.

Perry, Gray Thomas (b. 1898)

Trice, Patricia. "Gray Thomas Perry (b. 1898): Florida Pianist and Teacher." *The Bulletin of Historical Research in Music Education* 10 (July 1989): 85-105.

_____. "Gray Thomas Perry, Piano Performer and Pedagogue." Ph.D. diss., The Florida State University, 1988.

Pitts, Lilla Belle (1884-1970)

Blanchard, Gerald L. "Lilla Belle Pitts: Her Life and Contribution to Music Education." Ed.D. diss., Brigham Young University, 1966.

"In Memoriam: Lilla Belle Pitts." *Music Educators Journal* 56 (March 1970): 105.

The New Grove Dictionary of American Music, 1986 ed. S.v. "Pitts, Lilla Belle," by George N. Heller.

Playford, John (1623-1686)

Grashel. John W. "John Playford's *An Introduction to the Skill of Musick* and Its Influence on Musical Textbooks of Colonial America." *The Bulletin of Historical Research in Music Education* 5 (July 1984): 39-54.

Meyer, Ramon E. "John Playford's *An Introduction to the Skill of Music*." Ph.D. diss., The Florida State University, 1961.

Nelson, Russell C. "John Playford and the English Amateur Musician." Ph.D. diss., University of Iowa, 1966.

Pommer, William Henry (1851-1937)

Wenger, Janice. "William Henry Pommer: His Life and Works." D.M.A. diss., University of Missouri-Kansas City, 1987.

_____. "William Henry Pommer: Missouri Musician." *The Bulletin of Historical Research in Music Education* 12 (January 1991): 13-26.

Porter, Quincy (1897-1966)

Hall, Willard K. "Quincy Porter: His Life and Contributions as a Composer and Educator (1897-1966)." D.M.A. diss., University of Missouri, Kansas City, 1970.

The New Grove Dictionary of American Music, 1986 ed. S.v. "Porter, (William) Quincy," by Howard Boatwright.

Presser, Theodore (1848-1925)

Nazzaro, William J. "Theodore Presser and His Foundation." *Music Educators Journal* 70 (October 1983): 48-49, 61, 63, 65, 67.

The New Grove Dictionary of American Music, 1986 ed. S.v. "Presser, Theodore," by Warren Storey Smith.

Scholten, James W. Review of "Theodore Presser, Educator, Publisher, Philanthropist: Selected Contributions to the Music Teaching Profession in America" (Ed.D. diss., University of Illinois, 1978), by Chris Yoder. *Bulletin of the Council for Research in Music Education* 87 (Spring 1986): 54-57.

Yoder, Chris. "Theodore Presser, Educator, Publisher, Philanthropist: Selected Contributions to the Music Teaching Profession in America." Ed.D. diss., University of Illinois, 1978.

Prokofiev, Sergei (1891-1953)

Vernazza, Marcelle. "Prokofiev: Child Composer and Composer for Children." *The American Music Teacher* 34 (November-December 1984): 26-27.

Rapp, George (1757-1847)

Wetzel, Richard D. "The Music of George Rapp's Harmony Society, 1805-1906." Ph.D. diss., University of Pittsburgh, 1970.

Ravenscroft, Thomas

Stroud, William P. "The Ravenscroft Psalter (1621): The Tunes, with a Background on Thomas Ravenscroft and Psalm Singing in His Time." D.Mus.A. diss., University of Southern California, 1959.

Reimer, Bennett (b. 1932)

Aquino, John. "Reimer Revisited." *Music Educators Journal* 66 (November 1979): 40-43, 84-85.

The New Grove Dictionary of American Music, 1986 ed. S.v. "Reimer, Bennett," by George N. Heller.

Reinagle, Alexander (1756-1809)

Mahan, Katherine Hines. "Hopkinson and Reinagle: Patriot-Musicians of Washington's Time." *Music Educators Journal* 62 (April 1976): 40-50.

The New Grove Dictionary of American Music, 1986 ed. S.v. "Reinagle, Alexander," by Robert Hopkins.

Revelli, William D. (b. 1902)

Cavanaugh, George A. "William D. Revelli: The Hobart Years." Ed.D. diss., The University of Michigan, 1971.

Froelich, Hildegard. "William D. Revelli's Message to Music Educators." *Music Educators Journal* 75 (April 1989): 22-26.

Mark, Michael L. "William D. Revelli: Portrait of a Distinguished Career." *Journal of Band Research* 16 (Fall 1980): 1-28.

The New Grove Dictionary of American Music, 1986 ed. S.v. "Revelli, William D.," by George N. Heller.

Robertson, R. Richie (1869-1939)

Scott, Lori D. "R. Richie Robertson: His Influence on Music Education and Communit' Music." Master's thesis, The University of Kansas, 1987.

Robeson, Paul (1898-1976)

Dunn, Gloria F. "Paul Robeson's Career as a Musician: Implications for Music Education." Ph.D. diss., The University of Michigan, 1987.

Miller, Samuel D. Review of "Paul Robeson's Career as a Musician: Implications for Music Education" (Ph.D. diss., The University of Michigan, 1987), by Gloria Francis Dunn. In *Bulletin of the Council for Research in Music Education Bulletin* 101 (Summer 1989): 66-69.

The New Grove Dictionary of American Music, 1986 ed. S.v. "Robeson, Paul," by Max de Schauensee.

Rolland, Paul

Smith, G. Jean. "Pioneers in String Education: The Legacy of Paul Rolland." *The Instrumentalist* 40 (January 1987): 25-29.

Root, Frederick Woodman (1846-1916)

Heller, George N. "Frederick Woodman Root (1846-1916): Singing Teacher Extraordinaire." *Update* 5 (Spring 1987): 4-5.

The New Grove Dictionary of American Music, 1986 ed. S.v. "Root, Frederick W.," by William Osborne.

Root, George F. (1820-1895)

Carder, M. Pauline. "George Frederick Root, Pioneer Music Educator: His Contributions to Mass Instruction in Music." Ed.D. diss., University of Maryland, 1971.

The New Grove Dictionary of American Music, 1986 ed. S.v. "Root, George Frederick," by Dena J. Epstein, H. Wiley Hitchcock, and Polly Carder.

Root, George F. *The Story of a Musical Life: An Autobiography*. Cincinnati: The John Church Co., 1891.

Rush, Ralph E.

Smart, Ronald E. "Ralph E. Rush: A Biography." D.M.A. diss., University of Southern California, 1974.

Russianoff, Leon

Clark, Stephen L. "Leon Russianoff: Clarinet Pedagogue." D.M.A. diss., University of Oklahoma, 1983.

Samaroff [Stokowski], Olga (1881-1948)

Kline, Donna S. "Olga Samaroff: Teacher Extraordinaire." *American Music Teacher* 38 (June-July 1989): 10-15.

McGillen, Geoffrey E. "The Teaching and Artistic Legacy of Olga Samaroff Stokowski." D.A. diss. Ball State University, 1989.

The New Grove Dictionary of American Music, 1986 ed. S.v. "Samaroff, Olga," by John G. Doyle.

Pucciani, Donna. "Olga Samaroff (1881-1948): American Music Educator." Ph.D. diss., New York University, 1979.

Schelling, Ernest (1876-1939)

Hill, Thomas H. "Ernest Schelling (1876-1939): His Life and Contributions to Music Education Through Educational Concerts." D.M.A. diss., The Catholic University of America, 1970.

The New Grove Dictionary of American Music, 1986 ed. S.v. "Schelling, Ernest," by Katherine K. Preston.

Schmauk, Johann Gottfried (1790-1849)

Wolf, Edward C. "Johann Gottfried Schmauk: German-American Music Educator." *Journal of Research in Music Education* 25 (Summer 1977): 139-150.

Seashore, Carl E. (1866-1949)

Heller, George N. "Carl Emil Seashore and James Lockhart Mursell: The Famous Controversy—Did It Ever Exist?" *Update* 4 (Spring 1986): 13-14.

The New Grove Dictionary of American Music, 1986 ed. S.v. "Seashore, Carl E.," by Ramona H. Matthews.

Seeger, Ruth Crawford (1901-1953)

Gaume, Mary Matilda. "Ruth Crawford Seeger: Her Life and Works." Ph.D. diss., Indiana University, 1973.

The New Grove Dictionary of American Music, 1986 ed. S.v. "Crawford (Seeger), Ruth," by Matilda Gaume.

Wilding-White, Ray. "Remembering Ruth Crawford Seeger: An Interview with Charles and Peggy Seeger." *American Music* 6 (Winter 1988): 242-254.

Sharp, Cecil (1859-1924)

Cox, Gordon. "The Legacy of Folk Song: The Influence of Cecil Sharp on Music Education." *British Journal of Music Education* 7 (July 1990): 89-97.

The New Grove Dictionary of American Music, 1986 ed. S.v. "Sharp, Cecil," by Frank Howes.

Shaw, Robert (b. 1916)

Brasher, Earlene D. "The Contributions of Robert Shaw and the Atlanta Symphony Orchestra to the Educational and Cultural Climate of Atlanta." Ph.D. diss., University of Southern Mississippi, 1988.

The New Grove Dictionary of American Music, 1986 ed. S.v. "Shaw, Robrt," by Michael Steinberg and Dennis K, McIntire.

Showalter, Anthony J. (1858-1924)

Reed, Joel F. "Anthony J. Showalter (1858-1924): Southern Educator, Publisher, Composer." Ed.D. diss., New Orleans Baptist Theological Seminary, 1975.

The New Grove Dictionary of American Music, 1986 ed. S.v. "Showalter, A. J.," by Joel F. Reed.

Skilton, Charles Sanford (1868-1941)

The New Grove Dictionary of American Music, 1986 ed. S.v. "Skilton, Charles Sanford," by David E. Campbell.

Smith, James A. "Charles Sanford Skilton (1868-1941): Kansas Composer." Master's thesis, The University of Kansas, 1979.

Smith, Eleanor (1858-1942)

Alper, Clifford D. "The Early Childhood Song Books of Eleanor Smith: Their Affinity with the Philosophy of Friedrich Froebel." *Journal of Research in Music Education* 28 (Summer 1980): 111-118.

Smith, Fowler (b. 1885)

Beattie, John W. "Fowler Smith: Far-Sighted Administrator." *Music Educators Journal* 45 (April-May 1959): 51-54.

Smith, Gregg (b. 1931)

Mauldin, Walt. "The Influence of Gregg Smith on Twentieth-Century Choral Literature as a Composer and Conductor." D.M.A. diss., University of Miami, 1989.

_____. "The Influence of Gregg Smith on Twentieth-Century Choral Literature as a Composer and Conductor." *The Bulletin of Historical Research in Music Education* 12 (July 1991): 83-99.

The New Grove Dictionary of American Music, 1986 ed. S.v. "Smith, Gregg," by Dale Cockrell.

Smith, N. Clark (1877-1933)

Buckner, Reginald T. "Rediscovering Major N. Clark Smith." *Music Educators Journal* 71 (February 1985): 36-42.

The New Grove Dictionary of American Music, 1986 ed. S.v. "Smith, N. Clark," by Dominique-René de Lerma.

Snedden, David (1868-1951)

Lee, William R. "The Snedden-Farnsworth Exchanges of 1917 and 1918 on the Value of Music and Art Education." *Journal of Research in Music Education* 31 (Fall 1983): 203-213.

Spiller, Isabele Taliaferro (1888-1974)

Anderson, Phyllis Wynn, "Isabele Taliaferro Spiller: Harlem Music Educator." D.M.A. diss., University of Georgia, 1988.

_____. "Isabele Taliaferro Spiller: Harlem Music Educator, 1925-1958." *Georgia Music News* 51 (Fall 1990): 48-50.

Stewart, N. Coe (1837-1921)

Heller, George N. "Goals and Objectives for School Music: N. Coe Stewart's Topeka NEA Address of 1886." *Update* 2 (Spring 1984): 23-26.

Still, William Grant (1895-1978)

Headlee, Judith Anne Still. "William Grant Still: A Voice High-Sounding." *Music Educators Journal* 70 (February 1984): 24-30.

The New Grove Dictionary of American Music, 1986 ed. S.v. "Still, William Grant," by Eileen Southern.

Stock, Frederick (1872-1942)

Berglund, Donald H. "A Study of the Life and Work of Frederick Stock During the Time He Served as Musical Director of the Chicago Symphony Orchestra with Particular Reference to His Influence on Music Education." Ph.D. diss., Northwestern University, 1955.

The New Grove Dictionary of American Music, 1986 ed. S.v. "Stock, Frederick," by Michael Steinberg.

Surette, Thomas W. (1861-1941)

Heffernan, Charles W. "Thomas Whitney Surette: Musician and Teacher." Ph.D. diss., The University of Michigan, 1962.

The New Grove Dictionary of American Music, 1986 ed. "Whitney, Thomas Whitney," by William McClellan.

Suzuki, Shinichi

Zinar, Ruth. "Shinichi Suzuki: The Mother-Tongue Method." *The American Music Teacher* 34 (September-October 1984): 26-27.

Swan, Howard (b. 1906)

Fowler, Charles, ed. *Conscience of a Profession: Howard Swan, Choral Director and Teacher*. Chapel Hill, NC: Hinshaw Music, Inc., 1987.

Rasmussen, David A. "Howard Swan: Teacher and Conductor." Ed.D. diss. Arizona State University, 1989.

Swingle, Ward

Shannon, Kathleen M. "Ward Swingle: A Study of His Choral Music and Its Jazz Influences." D.M.A. diss., University of Miami, 1990.

Tapper, Thomas

The New Grove Dictionary of American Music, 1986 ed. S.v. "Tapper, Thomas," by William McClellan.

Remsen, Katherine G. "Thomas Tapper: His Contribution to Music Education." Ph.D. diss., The University of Michigan, 1975.

Thomas, Theodore (1835-1905)

The New Grove Dictionary of American Music, 1986 ed. S.v., "Thomas, Theodore," by Ezra Schabas.

Russell, Theodore C. "Theodore Thomas: His Role in the Development of Musical Culture in the United States, 1835-1905." Ph.D. diss., University of Minnesota, 1969.

Thurber, Jeanette Meyers (1850-1946)

The New Grove Dictionary of American Music, 1986 ed. S.v. "Thurber, Jeanette," by Emile H. Serposs.

Rubin, Emanuel. "Jeanette Meyers Thurber and the National Conservatory of Music." *American Music* 8 (Fall 1990): 294-325.

Tinker, Milton Z.

"Some Veteran Supervisors: Brief Sketches of W. A. Hogdon, B. Jepson, M. Z. Tinker, J. E. Bailey, and H. M. Butler." *School Music Monthly* 4 (May 1903): 9-16.

Tinker, Milton Z. "School Music in Indiana: Recollections of Early Days." *School Music* 9 (September 1908): 38-41.

Tipton, Gladys (b. 1905)

Bond, Dorothea M. "Gladys Tipton: Her Life and Contributions to Music Education as a Teacher, Author, and Clinician." Ph.D. diss., George Peabody College for Teachers of Vanderbilt University, 1987.

Tourjée, Eben (1834-1891)

The New Grove Dictionary of American Music, 1986 ed. S.v. "Tourjé, Eben," by Harry Eskew.

Tovey, Donald F. (1875-1940)

Whatley, George L. "Donald Francis Tovey and His Contributions to the Study of Harmony and Counterpoint." Ph.D. diss., Indiana University, 1974.

Tufts, Rev. John (1689-1750)

Finney, Theodore M. "The Third Edition of Tufts' *Introduction to the Art of Singing Psalm-Tunes*." *Journal of Research in Music Education* 14 (Fall 1966): 163-170.

Gates, J. Terry. "A Comparison of the Tune Books of Tufts and Walters." *Journal of Research in Music Education* 36 (Fall 1988): 169-193.

Lowens, Irving. "John Tufts' *Introduction to the Singing of Psalm Tunes* (1721-1744): The First American Music Textbook." *Journal of Research in Music Education* 2 (Fall 1954): 89-102.

The New Grove Dictionary of American Music, 1986 ed. S.v. "Tufts, John," by Nym Cooke.

Tuthill, Burnet C. (b. 1888)

Raines, Jean L. "Burnet C. Tuthill: His Life and Music." Ph.D. diss., Michigan State University, 1959.

The New Grove Dictionary of American Music, 1986 ed. S.v. "Tuthill, Burnet C.," by Robert Stevenson.

Weerts, Richard. Review of "Burnet C. Tuthill: His Life and Music" (Ph.D. diss., Michigan State University, 1959), by Jean L. Raines. *Bulletin of the Council for Research in Music Education* 70 (Spring 1982): 31-34.

Turner, William Wolcott (1800-1887)

Darrow, Alice-Ann, and George N. Heller. "Early Advocates of Music Education for the Hearing Impaired: William Wolcott Turner and David Ely Bartlett." *Journal of Research in Music Education* 33 (Winter 1985): 269-279.

Ursinus, Abraham (c. 1600)

Livingstone, Ernest F. "The Theory and Practice of Protestant School Music as Seen Through the Collection of Abraham Ursinus (c. 1600)." Ph.D. diss., The Eastman School of Music, University of Rochester, 1962.

van de Wall, Willem (1887-1953)

Heller, George N., and Alicia Ann Clair. "Willem van de Wall (1887-1953): Organizer and Innovator in Music Education and Music Therapy." *Journal of Research in Music Education* 37 (Fall 1989): 165-178.

Vandercook, H. A. (1864-1949)

The New Grove Dictionary of American Music, 1986 ed. S.v., "Vandercook H. A.," by Raoul Camus.

Wilson, Gilbert E. "H. A. Vandercook, the Teacher." D.M.A. diss., University of Missouri, Kansas City, 1970.

Venth, Carl (1860-1938)

Gibbs, Gary D. "Carl Venth (1860-1938): Texas Master Musician, His Life, His Music, His Influence." Ph.D. diss., University of Texas at Austin, 1990.

Villa-Lobos, Heitor (1884-1959)

Vassberg, David E. "Villa-Lobos as Pedagogue: Music in the Service of the State." *Journal of Research in Music Education* 23 (Fall 1975): 163-170.

Wagner, Roger (b. 1914)

Belan, William. "An Interview with Roger Wagner." *Choral Journal* 32 (August 1991): 7-16.

The New Grove Dictionary of American Music, 1986 ed. S.v. "Wagner, Roger," by Martin Bernheimer.

Walker, William (1809-1875)

Eskew, Harry. "William Walker's *Southern Harmony*: Its Basic Education." *Latin American Music Review* 7 (Fall-Winter 1986): 137-146.

The New Grove Dictionary of American Music, 1986 ed. S.v. "Walker, William," Harry Eskew.

Walter, Rev. Thomas (1696-1725)

Gates, J. Terry. "A Comparison of the Tune Books of Tufts and Walters." *Journal of Research in Music Education* 36 (Fall 1988): 169-193.

The New Grove Dictionary of American Music, 1986 ed. S.v. "Walter, Thomas," by Nym Cooke.

Fred Waring (1900-1984)

"In Memoriam . . . Fred Waring." *The Choral Journal* 25 (June 1985): 5.

The New Grove Dictionary of American Music, 1986 ed. S.v. "Waring, Fred," by Jean W. Thomas.

Weaver, Sterrie A.

Thompson, Cyrus. "Sterrie A. Weaver: His Life and Contribution to Music Education." Master's thesis, Eastman School of Music, University of Rochester, 1942.

Webster, Mary Cushing (1812-1905)

Grant, Francis. "Mary Cushing Webster: Pioneer Music Educator." *Journal of Research in Music Education* 14 (Summer 1966): 99-114.

Weiss, Julius

Albrecht, Theodore. "Julius Weiss: Scott Joplin's First Piano Teacher." *College Music Symposium* 19 (Fall 1979): 89-105.

Wiley, D. O.

Hansford, James A. "D. O. ('Prof') Wiley: His Contributions to Music Education (1921-1963)." Ph.D. diss., North Texas State University, 1982.

Lowe, Donald R. Review of "D. O. ('Prof') Wiley: His Contributions to Music Education (1921-1963)" (Ph.D. diss., North Texas State University, 1982), by James A. Hansford. *Bulletin of the Council for Research in Music Education* 84 (Fall 1985): 63-65.

Willems, Edgar (1890-1978)

Damaceno, Gerson G. "The Edgar Willems Approach to Music Education." D.M.E. diss., University of Cincinnati, 1965.

_____. "Personalities in World Music Education, No. 10—Edgar Willems." *International Journal of Music Education* 15 (1990): 39-44.

Williamson, John Finley (1887-1964)

The New Grove Dictionary of American Music, 1986 ed. S.v. "Williamson, John Finley," by Gene Biringer.

Wehr, David A. "John Finley Williamson (1887-1964): His Life and Contribution to Choral Music." Ph.D. diss., University of Miami, 1971.

Wolfe, Irving W.

Goss, Donald R. "Irving W. Wolfe: His Life and Contributions to Music Education." Ph.D. diss., George Peabody College for Teachers, 1972.

Woodbridge, William Channing (1794-1845)

Alcott, William. "William Channing Woodbridge." *American Journal of Education* 5 (June 1858): 51-64.

Biographical Dictionary of American Educators, 1978 ed. S.v., "Woodbridge, William Channing," by D. Richard Bowles.

Silantien, John J. "William Channing Woodbridge: His Life and Contributions to American Music Education." Master's thesis, The Catholic University of America, 1972.

Woodbury, Isaac Baker (1819-1858)

Copeland, Robert M. "The Life and Works of Isaac Baker Woodbury, 1819-1858." Ph.D. diss., University of Cincinnati, 1974.

Heller, George N. "Isaac Baker Woodbury (1819-1858) and Early Music Teacher Training." *Update* 6 (Spring 1988): 17-18.

Higginson, J. Vincent. "Isaac B. Woodbury (1818-1858)." *The Hymn* 20 (1969): 74-80.

The New Grove Dictionary of American Music, 1986 ed. S.v. "Woodbury, Isaac B.," by Robert M. Copeland.

Zimmerman, Frederick

Blumenthal, Jay S. "Frederick Zimmerman: Double Bass Performer and Pedagogue." Ph.D. diss., New York University, 1984.

II. GEOGRAPHICAL STUDIES

Eastern Division

Buechner, Alan C. "Yankee Singing Schools and the Golden Age of Choral Music in New England, 1760-1800." Ed.D. diss., Harvard University, 1960.

Gates, J. Terry. "Music Education's Professional Beginnings in America: Early Eighteenth-Century New England Singing School Teacher Qualifications and Program Goals." *The Quarterly* 1 (Spring 1990): 43-48.

Heller, George N. "Historical Research in Music Education: The Eastern Division of MENC." *Update* 9 (Fall-Winter 1990): 17-22.

Music, David W. "The Diary of Samuel Sewall and Congregational Singing in Early New England." *The Hymn* (January 1990): 7.

Rider, Daniel E. "The Musical Thought and Activities of the New England Transcendentalists." Ph.D. diss., University of Minnesota, 1964.

Osterhout, Paul R. "Note Reading and Regular Singing in Eighteenth-Century New England." *American Music* 4 (Summer 1986): 125-144.

Thompson, James W. "Music and Musical Activities in New England, 1800-1838." Ph.D. diss., George Peabody College for Teachers, Vanderbilt University, 1962.

Worst, John W. "New England Psalmody 1760-1810: Analysis of an American Idiom." Ph.D. diss., The University of Michigan, 1974.

Connecticut

Larsen, Arved M. "A History of the Connecticut Music Educators Association, 1933-1967." Ph.D. diss., The Florida State University, 1968.

Lieberman, Milton. "Development of Music in the Hartford, Connecticut Public Schools to Their Consolidation in 1934." Master's thesis, Hartt College of Music, 1951.

Noss, Luther. "Music Comes to Yale." *American Music* 3 (Fall 1985): 337-346.

Delaware

Maynard, Clarke. "Music Supervision in Wilmington, Delaware: The Story of a Ten-Year Enterprise." Ed.D. diss., Columbia University, 1958.

District of Columbia

Elward, Thomas J. "A History of Music Education in the District of Columbia Public Schools from 1845 to 1945." D.M.A. diss., The Catholic University of America, 1975.

Maine

Cole, Ronald F. "Music in Portland, Maine, from Colonial Times Through the Nineteenth Century." Ph.D. diss., Indiana University, 1975.

Maryland

Disharoon, Richard A. "A History of Municipal Music in Baltimore, 1914-1947." Ph.D. diss., University of Maryland, 1980.

Fisher, James L. "The Roots of Music Education in Baltimore." *Journal of Research in Music Education* 21 (Fall 1973): 214-224.

_____. "The Origin and Development of Public School Music in Baltimore to 1870." Ed.D. diss., University of Maryland, 1970.

Robinson, Ray E. "A History of the Peabody Conservatory of Music." Mus.Ed.D. diss., Indiana University, 1969.

_____. "The Peabody Institute: The Ideas Implicit in Its Founding." *Journal of Research in Music Education* 19 (Summer 1971): 216-221.

Schaaf, Elizabeth. "From Idea to Tradition: The Peabody Prep." *Music Educators Journal* 72 (September 1985): 38-43.

Taylor, Corwin H. *A History of the Maryland Music Educators Association: 1941-1977*. College Park, MD: The University of Maryland Press, 1978.

Massachusetts

Ayoob, Kenneth P. "An Annotated Bibliography of Original Works for Band Commissioned by or Composed for the Massachusetts Institute of Technology Concert Band Between 1952 and 1987." D.A. diss., University of Northern Colorado, 1988.

Brayley, A. W. "Early Instrumental Music in Boston." *The Bostonian* (November 1894): 189-195.

Fisher, William Arms. *Notes on Music in Old Boston*. Boston: Oliver Ditson, 1918.

Forbes, Elliott. *A History of Music at Harvard to 1972*. Cambridge, MA: Harvard University, Department of Music, 1988.

Hehr, Milton G. "Musical Activities in Salem, Massachusetts: 1783-1823." Ph.D. diss., Boston University, 1963.

Jorgenson, Estelle Z. "Engineering Change in Music Education: A Model of the Political Process Underlying the Boston School Music Movement (1829-1838)." *Journal of Research in Music Education* 31 (Spring 1983): 67-75.

Miller, David M. "The Beginnings of Music in the Boston Public Schools: Decisions of the Boston School Committee in 1837 and 1845 in Light of Religious and Moral Concerns of the Time." Ph.D. diss., University of North Texas, 1989.

Nitz, Donald A. "Community Musical Societies in Massachusetts to 1840." Mus.A.D. diss., Boston University, 1964.

Osterhout, Paul R. "Music in Northampton, Massachusetts to 1820." Ph.D. diss., The University of Michigan, 1978.

Paige, Paul P. "Musical Organizations in Boston: 1830-1850." Ph.D. diss., Boston University, 1967.

Rabin, Marvin J. "History and Analysis of the Greater Boston Youth Symphony Orchestra from 1958-1964." Ed.D. diss., University of Illinois, 1968.

Wilson, Bruce D. "A Documentary History of Music in the Schools of the City of Boston, 1830-1850." Ph.D. diss., The University of Michigan, 1973.

New Hampshire

Keggereis, Richard I. "The Handel Society of Dartmouth." *American Music* 4 (Summer 1986): 177-193.

Marchesseault, Sr. Anita. "Music Education in the Schools of Manchester, New Hampshire from 1850 to 1970." Mus.A.D. Diss., Boston University, 1972.

Moran, John E. "History and Development of the Music Festival in New Hampshire." Master's thesis, Boston University, 1951.

Pichierri, Louis. "Music in New Hampshire, 1623-1800." Ph.D. diss., Syracuse University, 1956.

New Jersey

Dackow, Sandy. "ASTA Superstars in New Jersey–Too Good to Be True." *Tempo* (May 1978): 7-11.

_____. "Fifty Years of Excellence: New Jersey All-State Orchestra Continues a Tradition." *Tempo* (November 1978): 10-15.

Kaufman, Charles H. "Music in New Jersey, 1655-1860: A Study of Musical Activity and Musicians in New Jersey from Its First Settlement to the Civil War." Ph.D. diss., New York University, 1974.

Schisler, Charles H. "A History of Westminster Choir College, 1926-1973." Ph.D. diss., Indiana University, 1976.

Woodworth, William H. "The Federal Music Project of the Works Progress Administration in New Jersey." Ed.D. diss., The University of Michigan, 1970.

New York

Arberg, Harold W. "Organizing the Music Department at Hofstra College." Ed.D. diss., Teachers College, Columbia University, 1949.

Bancroft, B. Richard. "The Historical Development of the Music Department of the State University College at Fredonia, New York." Ed.D. diss., New York University, 1972.

Barresi, Anthony L. "The History and Programs of the New York State Council on the Arts." Ph.D. diss., The University of Michigan, 1973.

Bristow, George F. "Music in the Public Schools of New York [City]." *MTNA Proceedings* (1885): 28-50.

Brown, Frank W. "The History of the Corning Philharmonic Orchestra and Its Current Role in Community Music Education in Corning, New York." Ed.D. diss., University of Illinois, 1973.

Claudson, William D. "The History of the Crane Department of Music, State University of New York, College at Potsdam, 1884-1964." Ph.D. diss., Northwestern University, 1965.

Cole, Edgar B. "The College of Fine Arts of Syracuse University, 1894-1922." Ph.D. diss., Syracuse University, 1957.

Egan, Robert F. "The History of the Music School of the Henry Street Settlement." Ph.D. diss., New York University, 1967.

Fowler, Charles. "The Crane School: One Hundred Years of Excellence." *Musical America* (February 1986): 6, 10, 14, 16.

Kogan, Judith. *Nothing But the Best: The Struggle for Perfection at the Juilliard School*. Reprint Ed. New York: Limelight Editions, 1989.

The New Grove Dictionary of American Music, 1986 ed. S.v. "Chautauqua and Lyceum," by Frederick Crane.

Parisi, Barbara. "The History of Brooklyn's Three Major Performing Arts Institutions: The Brooklyn Academy of Music, Brooklyn Center for the Performing Arts at Brooklyn College, and St. Ann's Center for Restoration and the Arts, Inc." Ph.D. diss., New York University, 1991.

Ramsey, Thomas L. "A Study of the County Music Educators Associations in the State of New York with Recommendations for Future Development." Ed.D. diss., Columbia University, 1964.

Reed, Larry W. "The History of the Department of Music and Music Education: Teachers College Columbia University—The Early Years, 1887-1939." Ed.D. diss., Teachers College, Columbia University, 1982.

Swift, Frederic Fay. *A History of the New York State School Music Association, 1932-1975*. Oneonta, NY: Swift-Dorr Publications, Inc., n.d. [1975].

Troth, Eugene W. "The Teacher Training Program in Music at Chautauqua Institution, 1905-1930." Ph.D. diss., The University of Michigan, 1959.

_____. "The Teacher Training Program in Music at Chautauqua Institution, 1905-1930." *Journal of Research in Music Education* 9 (Spring 1961): 37-46.

Volk, Terese, M. "The Growth and Development of Music Education in the Public Schools of Buffalo, New York, 1843-1988." *The Bulletin of Historical Research in Music Education* 9 (July 1988): 91-118.

Wells, Jeanette L. "History of the Music Festival at Chautauqua Institution from 1874-1957." Ph.D. diss., The Catholic University of America, 1958.

Pennsylvania

Cromer, Gladys. "The History and Growth of the Pennsylvania Music Educators Association." D.Ed. diss., The Pennsylvania State University, 1955.

Faulcon, Clarence. "A History of Musical Pennsylvania Before 1850." D.Mus., Philadelphia Conservatory of Music, 1962.

Fino, John M. "A Study of Changing Attitudes Between Past and Current Practices in General Music Instruction of Public Elementary and Secondary Schools of Pennsylvania, 1940-1975." D.M.A. diss., Temple University, 1979.

Fisher, Paul G. "Music: A Dominant Force in the First Century of Lebanon Valley College." Ed.D. diss, The University of Michigan, 1969.

Hahn, Ruth S. "Music and the Harmonists." *The Sonneck Society Bulletin* 14 (Fall 1988): 119-120.

Hall, Harry H. "The Moravian Wind Ensemble: Distinctive Chapter in America's Music." Ph.D. diss., George Peabody College for Teachers, 1967.

Hoople, Donald G. "Moravian Music Education and the American Moravian Music Tradition." Ed.D. diss., Columbia Teachers College, 1976.

Karjala, H. Eugene. Review of "Moravian Music Education and the American Moravian Music Tradition" (Ed.D. diss., Columbia Teachers College, 1976), by Donald Graham Hoople. *Bulletin of the Council for Research in Music Education* 61 (Winter 1980): 37-38.

Martin, Berry Jean. "The Ephrata Cloister and Its Music, 1732-1785: The Cultural, Religious, and Bibliographical Background." Ph.D. diss., University of Maryland, 1974.

Robertson, Yvonne A. "The Ephrata Cloister and the Lititz Moravian Settlement, 1732-1820, and a Comparative Study of Their Musical Cultures." D.M.A. diss., Juilliard School of Music, 1986.

Rosewall, Richard B. "Singing Schools of Pennsylvania, 1800-1900." Ph.D. diss., University of Minnesota, 1969.

Sims, Edward R. "The History of the Music Department of the Indiana University of Pennsylvania and Its Contribution to Music Education." Ed.D. diss., The University of Michigan, 1968.

Rhode Island

Vermont

Gary, Charles L. Review of *Music and Education in Vermont, 1700-1900*, by James A. Keene. In*Bulletin of the Council for Research in Music Education* 102 (Fall 1989): 95-96.

Keene, James A. "A History of Music Education in Vermont 1770-1900." Ph.D. diss., The University of Michigan, 1969.

_____. *Music and Education in Vermont, 1700-1900*. Macomb, IL: Glenbridge Publishing, Ltd., 1987.

_____. "Music Education in the Private Schools of Vermont in the Nineteenth Century." *Journal of Research in Music Education* 19 (Summer 1971): 195-203.

Kegerreis, Richard I. "The Handel Society of Dartmouth." *American Music* 4 (Summer 1986): 177-193.

North Central Division

Busche, Henry E. "The History of High School Choral Activities in Three Selected Cities of the United States." Ed.D. diss., University of Illinois, 1963.

Harper, Cyrus P. "The Early Development of Instrumental Music in Selected Public High Schools of Seven North Central States." Ph.D. diss., Northwestern University, 1953.

Hendricksen, David A. "Twentieth-Century Choral Music Programming by Concordia, Luther, and St. Olaf College Choirs, 1950-1986." D.A. diss., Ball State University, 1988.

Jachens, Darryl L. "The Pedagogical Approaches of Eight Important Midwestern Band Conductors During the Late 1920s and 1930s." *The Journal of Band Research* 22 (Spring 1987): 44-54.

Thompson, James W. "Music and Musical Activities in New England, 1800-1838." Ph.D. diss., George Peabody College for Teachers, 1962.

Illinois

Guion, David M. "From Yankee Doodle Thro' to Handel's Largo: Music at the World's Columbian Exposition." *College Music Symposium* 24 (Spring 1984): 81-96.

Harrison, Albert D. "A History of the University of Illinois School of Music, 1940-1970." Ed. D. diss., University of Illinois, 1986.

Lester, Paul F. "The Development of Music at the University of Illinois and a History of the School of Music." Master's thesis, University of Illinois, 1943.

Mathis, George R. "A Study of Music Teacher Preparation at Illinois Wesleyan University, 1930-1959." Ed.D. diss., University of Illinois, 1962.

McMullen, John R. "A History of Music in Aurora, Illinois" Ph.D. diss., Chicago Musical College, 1955.

Miller, Daniel T. "The Columbian Exposition of 1893 and the American National Character." *Journal of American Culture* 10 (Summer 1987): 17-22.

Mistak, Alvin F. "A General History of Instrumental Music in the Chicago Public Schools: 1900-1950." Ph.D. diss., The University of Iowa, 1969.

Podrovsky, Rosagitta. "A History of Music Education in the Chicago Public Schools." Ph.D. diss., Northwestern University, 1978.

Prince, Joe N. "An Evaluation of Graduate Programs at the University of Illinois," Ed.D. diss., University of Illinois, 1968.

Sanford, Gordon T. Review of "A History of the University of Illinois School of Music, 1940-1970" (Ed.D. diss., University of Illinois, 1986), by Albert D. Harrison. In *Bulletin of the Council for Research in Music Education* 102 (Fall 1989): 77-78.

Indiana

Anzalone, Felicie. "Development of School Music in Indiana." Master's Thesis, Northwestern University, 1943.

Burkhalter, Peter F. "Community Music in Berne, Indiana: Its Past and Future Development." Ed.D. diss., Columbia University, 1954.

Gary, Charles L. Review of "Music in New Harmony, Indiana, 1825 1865: A Study of the Music and Musical Activities of Robert Owen's Community of Equality and Its Cultural Afterglow" (Ph.D. diss., Indiana University, 1987), by Claude K. Sluder. In *Bulletin of the Council for Research in Music Education* 103 (Winter 1990): 68-71.

Meurer, Eleanor Kay. "An Evaluation of Music Teacher Education at Indiana State University, 1968-1972." Ed.D. diss., Indiana University, 1974.

Rothert, Harold H. "Growth and Development of Music Education in an Historic Town: Madison, Indiana (1892-1936)." Master's thesis, Indiana University, 1945.

Simpson, Edward L. "A Historical Study of Instrumental Music Education in Eight Selected High Schools in Indiana." Ed.D. diss., Indiana University, 1965.

Sluder, Claude K. "Music in New Harmony, Indiana, 1825-1865: A Study of the Music and Musical Activities of Robert Owen's Community of Equality (1825-1827) and Its Cultural Afterglow (1827-1865)." Ph.D. diss., Indiana University, 1987.

Tinker, Milton Z. "School Music in Indiana: Recollections of Early Days." *School Music* 9 (September 1908): 38-41.

Iowa

Benson, Robert J. "The Development of Music at Graceland College from 1895 to 1945." Ph.D. diss., Chicago Musical College, 1955.

Betterton, William F. "A History of Music in Davenport, Iowa, before 1900." Ph.D. diss., University of Iowa, 1962.

Bruner, Robert R. "A History of Music in Cedar Rapids, Iowa Before 1900." Ph.D. diss., University of Iowa, 1964.

Bunch, William F. "An Evaluation of the Ph.D. Curriculum in Music at the University of Iowa from 1931 to 1967." Ph.D. diss., The University of Iowa, 1969.

Cook, Thomas H. "A History of Music at Central College During the Nineteenth Century." D.A. diss., University of Northern Colorado, 1983.

Farlee, Lloyd W. "A History of the Church Music of the Amana Society, the Community of Pure Inspiration." Ph.D. diss., The University of Iowa, 1966.

Jones, Nathan E. "Music at Drake University, 1881-1931." Ed.D. diss., The University of Michigan, 1964.

McKee, William D. "A History of the Iowa High School Music Association." Master's thesis, University of Iowa, 1929.

Pine, Mary L. "A History of Music Contests in Iowa." Master's thesis, Northwestern University, 1941.

Tennant, Donald B. "The History of Public School Music in Iowa, 1900-1951: A Study Limited to Secondary Schools in Selected Cities of Over 15,000 Population." Ph.D. diss., University of Iowa, 1952.

Thorstenson, Marvin S. *A History of the First Century of the Iowa Music Teachers Association, 1885-1985*. Iowa City, IA: Iowa Music Teachers Association, 1985.

Michigan

Austin, Henry R. "History of Broadcasting at the National Music Camp, Interlochen, Michigan, 1928-1958." Ed.D. diss., The University of Michigan, 1959.

Bartner, Arthur C. "The Charles Stewart Mott Foundation: Its Contributions to the Music Environment of Flint, Michigan (1935-1970)." Ed.D. diss., The University of Michigan, 1971.

Boggs, Jon W. "Music Instruction in Detroit from 1874 to 1929." Ph.D. diss., The University of Michigan, 1970.

Collins, Verne E. "Music in Ann Arbor High School." Ph.D. diss., The University of Michigan, 1966.

Crawford, Richard. "Music at Michigan: A Historical Perspective." In *100 Years of Music at Michigan: 1880-1980*. Ann Arbor, MI: The University of Michigan, 1979.

House, James B. "A History of the Michigan School Band and Orchestra Association: The First Twenty-Five Years, 1934-1959." Ed.D. diss., The University of Michigan, 1969.

Kegerreis, Richard I. "Flint Central Launches the High School A Cappella Choral Movement." *Journal of Research in Music Education* 14 (Winter 1966): 254-265.

Law, Arlene Sandra. "From Morality to Patriotism: The Role of School Music in Nineteenth-Century Detroit." Ph.D. diss., The University of Michigan, 1988.

Maybee, Harper C., Jr. "The of the Music Education Curriculum in the State Colleges of Education in Michigan, 1890-1950." Master's thesis, The University of Michigan, 1950.

Poland, Alan B. "A History of the Dow Chemical Company Music Department." Ph.D. diss., Michigan State University, 1976.

Schrader, Shirley L. "A History of the University Musical Society of Ann Arbor, Michigan, 1872-1892." Ph.D. diss., The University of Michigan, 1968.

Stegath, William B. "Radio Broadcasting at The University of Michigan, 1922-1958." Ph.D. diss., The University of Michigan, 1961.

Teal, Mary E. "Musical Activities in Detroit from 1701 Through 1870." Ph.D. diss., The University of Michigan, 1964.

Minnesota

Fergus, Patricia M. "Factors Affecting the Development of the Orchestra and String Programs in Minnesota Secondary Schools, 1940-1960." *Journal of Research in Music Education* 12 (Fall 1964): 235-243.

_____. "Factors Affecting the Development of the Orchestra and String Programs in Minnesota Secondary Schools, 1940-1960." Ph.D. diss., University of Minnesota, 1960.

Johnson, James R. "The Change in Status of Public School String Programs in Minnesota Between the Schools Years 1959-60 and 1967-68." Ed.D. diss., University of Illinois, 1969.

Kleinsasser, Jerome S. "Nineteenth-Century Twin City Choral Activities." Ph.D. diss., University of Minnesota, 1972.

LeGault, Maurice E. "A Descriptive Survey of the Choral Music Programs in Five Minneapolis High Schools During the Years 1925-1945." Ph.D. diss., University of Minnesota, 1969.

Parker, Linda F. "Women in Music Education in St. Paul, Minnesota from 1898 to 1957." *The Bulletin of Historical Research in Music Education* 8 (July 1987): 83-90.

_____. "Women in Music in St. Paul from 1898 to 1957 with Emphasis on the St. Paul Public Schools." Ph.D. diss., University of Minnesota, 1983.

Nebraska

MacDonald, Mildred A. "Music at Boys' Town, 1917-1970." Ph.D. diss., University of Colorado, 1972.

Mendyk, Leander A. "History of the Nebraska Music Educators Association, 1937-1967." Ed.D. diss., Colorado State College, 1969.

North Dakota

Ohio

Barber, Richard E. "A Comparison of the History of the Departments of Music at the University of Toledo, Findlay College, and Bowling Green State University." Ph.D. diss., The University of Michigan, 1976.

Bianco, Robert S. "The Secondary School Band Competition Festival in the State of Ohio from 1924 to 1969." Ed. D. diss., University of Cincinnati, 1970.

Campbell, William J. "A History of the Conservatory of Music, Baldwin-Wallace College, 1913-1970." Ed.D. diss., The University of Michigan, 1971.

Ebertz, Sr. Mary Joeling. "A History of the Development of Music Education in the Archdiocese of Cincinnati." Ed.D. diss., University of Cincinnati, 1955

Ellis, Frank R. "Music in Cincinnati." *MTNA Proceedings* (1913): 7-15.

Gary, Charles L. "A History of Music Education in the Cincinnati Public Schools." Ed.D. diss., University of Cincinnati, 1951.

_____. "A History of Music Education in the Cincinnati Public Schools." *Journal of Research in Music Education* 2 (Spring 1954): 11-20.

Grant, Francis H. "Foundations of Music Education in the Cleveland Public Schools." Ed.D. diss., Western Reserve University, 1963.

Harris, Charles W. "The Development of a Music Department in the University of Toledo." Master's thesis, The Ohio State University, 1948.

Kapfer, Miriam B. "Early Elementary School Bands in Columbus, Ohio, and the Columbian Celebration of 1892." *The Journal of Band Research* 5 (Autumn 1968): 4-7.

_____. "Early Public School Music in Columbus, Ohio, 1845-1854." *Journal of Research in Music Education* 15 (Fall 1967): 191-200.

_____. "Music Instruction and Supervision in the Public Schools of Columbus, Ohio from 1845 to 1900." Ph.D. diss., The Ohio State University, 1964.

Lewis, John. "An Historical Study of the Origin and Development of the Cincinnati Conservatory of Music." Ed.D. diss., University of Cincinnati, 1943.

McCowen, Edward. "The History and Development of Public School Music in Scioto County, Ohio." Master's thesis, Northwestern University, 1942.

Mitchell. Homer. "The Eisteddfod in Ohio." Master's thesis, The Ohio State University, 1943.

Orlando, Vincent A. "An Historical Study of the Origin and Development of the College of Music of Cincinnati." Ed.D. diss., University of Cincinnati, 1946.

Skyrm, Richard D. "Oberlin Conservatory: A Century of Musical Growth and Influence." D.Mus.A. diss., University of Southern California, 1962.

South Dakota

Asbaugh, Harold B. "A History of the Music Contest in South Dakota." Master's thesis, University of South Dakota, 1950.

Wisconsin

Busch, Stephen E. "A History of the Lawrence Conservatory of Music." Ed.D. diss., The University of Michigan, 1961.

Fonder, Mark. "Early School Music Instruction in Wisconsin." *The Bulletin of Historical Research in Music Education* 9 (July 1988): 79-80.

_____. "An Investigation of the Origin and Development of Four Wisconsin High School Bands." Ed.D. diss., University of Illinois, 1983.

_____. "The Wisconsin School Music Association and Its Music Contests: The Early Years." *Journal of Research in Music Education* 37 (Summer 1989): 112-131.

Kock, Marvin H. "Music Teacher Training in the Public Normal Schools of Wisconsin: A History Focused on the School at Milwaukee." Ph.D. diss., Northwestern University, 1975.

Riley, Martha Chrisman. Review of "A History of the Development of Milwaukee Public School Arts Policy from 1870 to 1930" (Ph.D. diss., University of Wisconsin-Milwaukee, 1984), by Aaria Butler Troiano. *Bulletin of the Council for Research in Music Education Bulletin* 94 (Fall 1987): 72-75.

Troiano, Aaria Butler. "A History of the Development of Milwaukee Public School Arts Policy from 1870 to 1930." Ph.D. diss., University of Wisconsin-Milwaukee, 1984.

Udell, Susan S. "An Historical/Descriptive Study of the Wisconsin Arts Board and Its Involvement in Arts Education." Ph.D. diss., University of Wisconsin, 1990.

Northwestern Division

Alaska

Idaho

Montana

Cowan, John R., Jr. "A History of the School of Music, Montana State University (1895-1952)." Master's thesis, University of Montana, 1952.

Oregon

Koehler, Herman R. "A Study of Factors Related to the Mission of the University of Oregon School of Music from 1964 to 1973." Ph.D. diss., University of Oregon, 1974.

Miller, Howard F. "The History and Present Trends of Inter-School Music Competition in the High Schools of Oregon." Master's thesis, University of Oregon, 1953.

Weddle, John W. "Early Bands of the Mid-Willamette Valley, 1850-1920." D.M.A. diss., University of Oregon, 1989.

Washington

Wyoming

Southern Division

Bess, David M. "A History of Comprehensive Musicianship in the Contemporary Music Project's Southern Region Institutes for Music in Contemporary Education." Ph.D. diss., West Virginia University, 1988.

_____. "Comprehensive Musicianship in the Contemporary Music Project's Southern Region Institutes for Music in Contemporary Education." *Journal of Research in Music Education* 39 (Summer 1991): 101-112.

Ellerbe, Marion F. "The Music Missionary of the Southern Baptist Convention: His Preparation and His Work." D.M.A. diss., The Catholic University of America, 1970.

Ellington, Charles L. "The Sacred Harp Tradition of the South: Its Origin and Evolution." Ph.D. diss., The Florida State University, 1969.

May, William V. Review of *Southern Music/American Music*, by Bill C. Malone. *The Bulletin of Historical Research in Music Education* 1 (July 1980): 17-18.

Alabama

Anderson, Fletcher C. "A History of Choral Music in Birmingham, Alabama." Ed.D. diss., University of Georgia, 1978.

Dorough, Prince L. "A History of the University of Montevallo Department of Music, 1918-1984." Ed.D. diss., University of Illinois, 1986.

Kennedy, Robert A. "A History and Survey of Community Music in Mobile, Alabama." Ed.D. diss., The Florida State University, 1968.

Florida

Copeland, Carolyn V. "The Contemporary Music Project in Florida." Ph.D. diss., The University of Michigan, 1976.

Crabb, Eugene N. "The High School Orchestra as an Integral Part of the Music Curriculum in Florida, 1900-1957." D.Mus.A. diss., University of Southern California, 1959.

Dahlenberg, "Music in the Culture of Miami: 1920-1966." Ed.D. diss., The Florida State University, 1967.

Doughty, Clinton. "The Development of the High School Band and Orchestra in Dade County, Florida." Master's thesis, University of Miami, 1953.

Heller, George N. Review of *A History of Music and Dance in Florida, 1565-1865* Wiley L. Housewright. *The Bulletin of Historical Research in Music Education* 13 (January 1992): 55-57.

Housewright, Wiley L. *A History of Music and Dance in Florida, 1565-1865*. Tuscaloosa, AL: University of Alabama Press, 1991.

Malone, Jacqui. "The FAMU Marching Band." *The Black Perspective in Music* 18 (1990): 59-80.

Royce, Leth M. "Survey of Music Education in Florida Secondary Schools." Master's thesis, The Florida State University, 1949.

Stone, Thomas J. "The Florida State Music Teachers Association, 1934-1956." Ph.D. diss., The Florida State University, 1957.

Swingle, Marilyn R. "A History of the Florida State University School of Music." Ph.D. diss., The Florida State University, 1973.

Whiteside, Thomas L. "A History of the Florida Music Educators Association and Its Component Organizations." Ph.D. diss., The Florida State University, 1970.

Williams, Grier M. "A History of Music in Jacksonville, Florida from 1822 to 1922." Ph.D. diss., The Florida State University, 1961.

Georgia

Broucek, Jack W. "Eighteenth-Century Music in Savannah, Georgia." Ed.D. diss., The Florida State University, 1963.

Davidson, Anderson. "The History of a Major Educational Influence: The University of Georgia Band." Master's thesis, University of Georgia, 1962.

Deen, Hugh G. "A Study of Public School Music in the State of Georgia." Master's thesis, University of Georgia, 1949.

Folds, Frank E. "The University of Georgia Redcoat Band." Master's thesis, University of Georgia, 1981.

Hoogerwerf, Frank W., ed. *Music in Georgia*. New York: Da Capo Press, 1984.

Lawson, Charles T. "Musical Life in the Unitas Fratrum Mission at Springplace, Georgia, 1800-1936." Ph.D. diss., The Florida State University, 1970.

Mahan, Katherine H. "History of Music in Columbus, Georgia, 1828-1928." Ph.D. diss., The Florida State University, 1967.

Steinhaus, Walter E. "Music in the Cultural Life of Macon, Georgia, 1823-1900." Ph.D. diss., The Florida State University, 1973.

Williford, Betty L. "A History of Music Education in the Public School of Atlanta, Georgia." Master's thesis, University of Georgia, 1966.

Kentucky

Berkey, Mildred. "A History of the New KMEA History." *Bluegrass Music News* 41 (May 1991): 14-15, 35.

Carle, David N. "A History of the School of Church Music of the Southern Baptist Theological Seminary, 1944-1959." D.M.A. diss., The Southern Baptist Theological Seminary, 1986.

Chambers, Virginia. "The Hindman Settlement School and Its Music." *Journal of Research in Music Education* 21 (Summer 1973): 135-144.

_____. "Music in Four Kentucky Mountain Settlement Schools." Ph.D. diss., The University of Michigan, 1970.

Chrisman, Martha C. "Popular Songs of the Genteel Tradition: Their Influence on Music Education in Public Schools of Louisville, Kentucky from 1850 to 1880." Ph.D. diss., University of Minnesota, 1985.

Forbes, John M. "The Music Program of Berea College (Kentucky) and the Folk-Music Heritage of Appalachia." Ph.D. diss., The University of Michigan, 1974.

Graham, John R. "Early Twentieth-Century Singing Schools in Kentucky Appalachia." *Journal of Research in Music Education* 19 (Spring 1971): 77-84.

Klein, Nancy Kirkland. "The Roots and Development of Public School Music in the State of Kentucky." Ph.D. diss., New York University, 1986.

Lewis, Eileen. "The Origin and Development of Music Festivals in Kentucky." Master's thesis, Northwestern University, 1943.

Parker, Joseph D. "A History of the Kentucky Music Educators Association, 1907-1981." D.M.A. diss., University of Kentucky, 1982.

Parker, Joseph D., and Mildred Berkey. *A History of the Kentucky Music Educators Association, 1907-1981 with an Addendum Through 1990*. Louisville, KY: The Kentucky Music Educators Association, 1991.

Riley, Martha Chrisman. "Portrait of a Nineteenth-Century School Music Program." *Journal of Research in Music Education* 38 (Summer 1990): 79-89.

West, Virginia B. "A History of Vocal Music in the Louisville Public Schools from 1900 to 1950." Master's thesis, University of Louisville, 1953.

Louisiana

Breen, Kermit T. "A History of the Shreveport Symphony Society from 1948 to 1967." Ph.D. diss., The Florida State University, 1970.

Burnham, Ray. "The History of Music Festivals in Louisiana, 1932-1966." Master's thesis, Northwestern Louisiana State College, 1966.

Herring, William J. "Music Education in the Public High Schools of Louisiana." Ph.D. diss., University of Southern Mississippi, 1973.

Price, Robert B. "A History of Music in Northern Louisiana Until 1900." D.M.A. diss., The Catholic University of America, 1977.

Roberts, Charlie W. "The History of the Louisiana State University School of Music." Ed.D. diss., The Louisiana State University, 1968.

Williams, Brenda G. "A History of the Louisiana State University School of Music (1955-1979)." Ph.D. diss., The Louisiana State University, 1983.

Mississippi

Angstadt, Albert W. "A History of Stage Bands in Mississippi's Secondary Schools Prior to April 1962." Master's thesis, University of Southern Mississippi, 1965.

Coats, Edsel R. "The Singing School in Mississippi, 1870-1964." Master's thesis, University of Southern Mississippi, 1965.

Dennis, Perry B. "A History of the Mississippi Music Educators Association." Mus.Ed.D. diss., University of Southern Mississippi, 1973.

Ferguson, James S. "A History of Music in Vicksburg, Mississippi." Ed.D. diss, The University of Michigan, 1970.

Green, Doris B. "A History of Music Education in the Elementary Schools of Mississippi Since 1900." Master's thesis, University of Southern Mississippi, 1964.

McKay, Sidney J. "Secondary One-Grade Schools in Mississippi: A Study of the Effects of 'Alexander et al. v. Holmes County Board of Education et al. (1969)' on Instrumental Music." Mus.Ed.D. diss., University of Southern Mississippi, 1975.

North Carolina

Anderson, Thomas J. "The Collegium Musicum Salem, 1780-1790: Origins and Repertoire." Ph.D. diss., The Florida State University, 1976.

Ater, Elma L. "A Historical Study of the Singing Conventions of the Indians of Robeson County, North Carolina." Master's thesis, The Ohio State University, 1943.

Culbertson, Anne E. "Music and Dance at the John C. Campbell Folk School in Brasstown, North Carolina, 1925-1985." D.Mus.Ed., diss., Indiana University, 1985.

Gates, J. Terry. Review of "Music in Antebellum Wilmington and the Lower Cape Fear of North Carolina" (Ph.D. diss., University of Colorado, 1979), by W. R. Ping. *Bulletin of the Council for Research in Music Education* 70 (Spring 1982): 52-54.

Hall, Harry H. "The Moravian Wind Ensemble: Distinctive Chapter in America's Music." Ph.D. diss., George Peabody College for Teachers, 1967.

Hines, Anna M. "Music at Black Mountain College: A Study of Experimental Ideas in Music." D.M.A. diss., University of Missouri, Kansas City, 1973.

Hoople, Donald G. "Moravian Music Education and the American Moravian Music Tradition." Ed.D. diss., Columbia Teachers College, 1976.

Karjala, H. Eugene. Review of "Moravian Music Education and the American Moravian Music Tradition" (Ed.D. diss., Columbia Teachers College, 1976), by Donald Graham Hoople. *Bulletin of the Council for Research in Music Education* 61 (Winter 1980): 37-38.

Kimel, Doris E. "A Study of the Changing Role of the Music Specialist in North Carolina Elementary Schools, 1950-1957." Master's thesis, Appalachian State University, 1958.

Marsh, Margaret T. "Music Education in the Public Schools of Greensboro, North Carolina, 1920-1967." Master's thesis, University of North Carolina at Greensboro, 1967.

McKinney, Jane G. "Developmental Pursuits of Excellence in North Carolina Music Education Shared by Alice Bivins, Grace VanDyke More, and Birdie Holloway During Their Careers at the University of North Carolina at Greensboro (1917-1965)." Ed.D. diss., University of North Carolina at Greensboro, 1989.

Miller, Thomas W. "Comprehensive Musicianship at East Carolina University, 1966-68." *The Quarterly* 1 (Autumn 1990): 58-60.

Mitchell, Joseph T. "Black Music in the University System of North Carolina: 1960-1974." Ed.D. diss., The University of North Carolina at Greensboro, 1975.

Pearsall, Howard T. "The North Carolina Symphony Orchestra from 1932 to 1962: Its Founding, Musical Growth, and Musical Activities." Mus.Ed.D. diss., Indiana University, 1969.

Ping, W. R. "Music in Antebellum Wilmington and the Lower Cape Fear of North Carolina." Ph.D. diss., University of Colorado, 1979.

Rierson, Charles F. "The Collegium Musicum Salem: The Development of a Catalogue of Its Library and the Editing of Selected Works." Ed.D. diss., University of Georgia, 1973.

Rothrock, Donna. "Moravian Music Education: Forerunner to Public School Music." *The Bulletin of Historical Research in Music Education* 8 (July 1987): 63-82.

Russell, Florita P. "A Historical Study of the Growth of Public School Music in North Carolina." Master's thesis, North Carolina College at Durham, 1955.

Swindell, June T. "Secondary Music Education for Negroes in the Public Schools of Raleigh, North Carolina, 1924-1966." Master's thesis, University of North Carolina at Greensboro, 1967.

Witherington, Joyce. "Teacher Training in Music at the University of North Carolina at Greensboro, 1891-1966." Master's thesis, University of North Carolina at Greensboro, 1966.

South Carolina

Bagdon, Robert J. "Musical Life in Charleston, South Carolina from 1632 to 1776 as Recorded in Colonial Sources." Ph.D. diss., University of Miami, 1978.

Turner, Daniel L. "Fundamentalism, the Arts, and Personal Refinement: A Study of the Ideals of Bob Jones, Sr., and Bob Jones, Jr." Ed.D. diss., University of Illinois, 1988.

Tennessee

Crain, Charles R. "Music Performance and Pedagogy in Nashville, Tennessee, 1818-1900." Ph.D. diss., George Peabody College for Teachers, 1975.

Crews, Emma K. "A History of Music in Knoxville, Tennessee, 1791 to 1910." Ed.D. diss., The Florida State University, 1961.

Dortch, Clarence W. "The Development of an A Cappella Choir at the Southern Missionary College, Collegedale, Tennessee." Master's thesis, North Texas State University, 1946.

Hancock, Paul C. "A History of Music Education in Nashville and Davidson County Public Schools (1873-1975): Local Reflections on National Practices in Music Education." Ed.D. diss. George Peabody College for Teachers, 1977.

Heller. George N. Review of "A History of Music Education in Nashville and Davidson County Public Schools (1873-1975): Local Reflections on National Practices in Music Education" (Ed.D. diss., George Peabody College for Teachers, 1977), by Paul C. Hancock. *Council for Research in Music Education Bulletin* 69 (Winter 1982): 40-42.

McDaniel, Walter. "A History of the Competition-Festival Movement in Instrumental Music in Middle Tennessee." Master's thesis, University of Tennessee, 1967.

Petree, Colbert G. "A Survey of the History of Music and Music Education at the University of Tennessee." Master's thesis, University of Tennessee, 1966.

Virginia

Darling, James F., and Maureen M. Wiggins. "A Constant Tuting–The Music of Williamsburg." *Music Educators Journal* 61 (November 1974): 56-61.

Eskew, Harry L. "Shape-Note Hymnody in the Shenandoah Valley, 1816-1860." Ph.D. diss., Tulane University, 1966.

Hancock, Lewis P. "The History of Public School Music in Virginia." Ed.D. diss., University of Virginia, 1963

Hines, James R. "Musical Activity in Norfolk, Virginia, 1680-1973." Ph.D. diss., The University of North Carolina at Chapel Hill, 1974.

Olson, Ivan W. "Music and Germans in Nineteenth-Century Richmond." *Journal of Research in Music Education* 14 (Spring 1966): 27-32.

_____. "The Roots and Development of Public School Music in Richmond, Virginia, 1782-1907." Ed.D. diss., The University of Michigan, 1964.

Ryder, William H. "Music at Virginia State College, 1883-1966." Ph.D. diss., The University of Michigan 1970.

Smith, Vernon L. "The Hampton Institute Choir, 1873-1973." Ph.D. diss., The Florida State University, 1985.

Stoutamire, Albert L. "A History of Music in Richmond, Virginia from 1742 to 1865." Ed.D. diss., The Florida State University, 1960.

West Virginia

Clark, Robert R. "The History of Music at Marshall University, Huntington, West Virginia: 1837-1970." Ph.D. diss., The University of Michigan, 1972.

Scarton, Richard J. "History of Music Education in West Virginia, 1880-1933." Master's thesis, University of West Virginia, 1962.

West, Owen L. "A History of the Influence of Certain Organizations, Agencies, and Individuals on Music Education in West Virginia, 1933-1963." Ph.D. diss., West Virginia University, 1966.

Southwestern Division

Cady, Henry. "Music in the Liberal Arts Colleges of Kansas and Missouri: An Investigation of Mutations in Philosophy from 1900 to 1960." Ph.D. diss., The University of Kansas, 1962.

Spell, Lota M. "Musical Education in North America During the Sixteenth and Seventeenth Centuries." Ph.D. diss., University of Texas, 1923.

Arkansas

Dalton, Ulysses G. "The Music Department of the University of Arkansas at Pine Bluff: Its Development and Role in Music Education in the State of Arkansas, 1873-1973." Ph.D. diss., The University of Michigan, 1981.

Colorado

Beier, David H. "Bands at the University of Colorado: An Historical Review, 1908-1978." Ph.D. diss., University of Colorado, 1983.

DeuPree, Donald D. "An Analysis of the Colorado Large-Group Music Competition-Festival System." Ed.D. diss., Colorado State College, 1968.

Flanders, Robert O. "The Contributions of Selected Music Educators to Instrumental Music Programs in the Public Schools of Colorado." Ed.D. diss., Colorado State College, 1965.

Fuller, James E. "Colorado Adult Amateur Bands and the Implications for Music Educators." Ed.D. diss., The University of Iowa, 1976.

James, Robert S. "History of Music in Greeley, Colorado, 1870-1920." Ed.D. diss., Colorado State College, 1967.

Klausman, Grant J. "A History of the University of Colorado College of Music." Ph.D. diss., University of Colorado, 1967.

Linscome, Sanford A. "A History of Musical Development in Denver, Colorado, 1858-1908." D.M.A. diss., The University of Texas, 1970.

Thelen, Charles C. "A Career Analysis of Selected Leading Colorado Music Educators since 1945." Ed.D. diss., University of Northern Colorado, 1973.

Kansas

Adamson, Elby. "A Family Tradition: Good Things Come in Threes." *Kansas Music Review* 52 (September 1990): 12.

Barkis, Betty J. "Methods of Reporting Pupil Progress in the Vocal Music Class in Kansas Elementary Schools." Master's thesis, The University of Kansas, 1955.

Bergee, Martin J. "A History of Music Education at The University of Kansas from 1947-1955." Master's thesis, The University of Kansas, 1984.

Buckner, Reginald T. "A History of Music Education in the Black Community of Kansas City, Kansas, 1905-1954." Ph.D. diss., University of Minnesota, 1974.

_____. "A History of Music Education in the Black Community of Kansas City, Kansas, 1905-1954." *Journal of Research in Music Education* 30 (Summer 1982): 91-106.

Clark, J. Bunker. *Music at KU: A History of the University of Kansas Music Department.* Lawrence, KS: The University of Kansas, 1986.

Copley, Elmer W. "A Comprehensive Performance Project in Solo Vocal Literature with an Essay: Messiah on the Plains, 1882-1976. A History of the Bethany Oratorio Society." D.M.A. Diss., The University of Iowa, 1976.

Coulson, Janet. "A History of the Fine Arts School at the University of Kansas." Master's thesis, The University of Kansas, 1941.

Crabb, J. Milford. "A History of Music in Kansas City, 1900-1965." D.M.A. diss., University of Missouri, Kansas City, 1967.

Crapson, Leland D. "Kansas Music Educators Association: The Establishment, Development, and Philosophy of Music Education." Ed.D. diss., Colorado State Teachers College, 1964.

Crawford, Loren. "A Survey of Music in the Church-Supported Colleges and Universities of the State of Kansas." Master's thesis, Eastman School of Music, University of Rochester, 1939.

Dalke, Jacob J. "A History of Music Education at the University of Kansas from 1936-1947." Master's thesis, The University of Kansas, 1980.

Donmeyer, Byron C. "Recent Trends with Reference to Music in Kansas High Schools." Master's thesis, The University of Kansas, 1933.

Dudley, Cathy H. "The History of Vocal Music in the Blue Valley Public Schools." Master's thesis, The University of Kansas, 1990.

Eiland, Diana K. "A History of the University of Kansas Band from 1878 to 1934." Master's thesis, The University of Kansas, 1984.

Elliott, Suzanne H. "The History of the Music Program in the Public Schools of the Rosedale District of Kansas City, Kansas, 1872-1973." Master's thesis, The University of Kansas, 1989.

Foerschler, Rebecca A. "A History of Choral Music Activity at The University of Kansas, 1866-1950." Master's thesis, The University of Kansas, 1989.

Geoffroy, Kenneth. "A Survey of Music Department Budgetary Practices and Procedures in Selected Kansas High Schools." Master's thesis, The University of Kansas, 1950.

Haack, Paul A., and George N. Heller. "Music, Education, and Community in Nineteenth-Century Kansas: Euterpe, Tönnies, and the Academy on the Plains." *Journal of Research in Music Education* 31 (Summer 1983): 115-132.

Harrell, Wynne J. "A History of Music Education in the Wichita, Kansas, Public Schools from 1871 to 1965." D.M.A. diss., University of Missouri, Kansas City, 1967.

Heller, George N. "'If You Come, Bring All Your Music': Music Education in Kansas Protestant Missions, 1830-1865." *Kansas Music Review* 45 (February 1983): 44-45.

_____. "Jesuit Missions in Kansas: Catholic Music Education, 1836-1871." *Kansas Music Review* 45 (March-April 1983): 12-14, 20.

_____. "KMEA During the War Years." *Kansas Music Review* 47 (December 1984): 12-13.

_____. "Kansas in NEA Music Education." *Kansas Music Review* 46 (March-April 1984): 16-17.

_____. "The Kansas Music Educators Association: Inception and the Early Years." *Kansas Music Review* 47 (September 1984): 12-14.

_____. "Music Education Among Native Americans in Kansas." *Kansas Music Review* 44 (September 1982): 16-17.

_____. "Music Education in the Kansas Territory: Settlement and Struggle, 1854-1865." *Kansas Music Review* 45 (September 1983): 18-20.

_____. "Music in Kansas Grade Schools from 1870 to 1900: A Study of Organization and Growth." *American Music* 3 (Winter 1985): 460-466.

_____. "Music Teacher Associations in Kansas, 1860-1899: Getting Organized." *Kansas Music Review* 46 (February 1984): 11, 31, 33, 36, 38, 41.

Jenson, Byron W. "College Music on the Konza Prairie: A History of Kansas State's Department of Music from 1863 to 1990." Ph.D. diss., Kansas State University, 1991.

Kirchoff, Kim A. "A History of Music Education at The University of Kansas from 1866 to 1936." Master's thesis, The University of Kansas, 1976.

Laneer, Larry P. "Marshall's Band of Topeka: A Study of the Golden Age of Bands in Topeka." Master's thesis, The University of Kansas, 1978.

Littrell, David. "The Kansas State University Orchestra." *Kansas Music Review* 52 (November 1990): 19.

McCarty, Diane M. "The History of Public School Music in Baldwin City, Kansas." Master's thesis, The University of Kansas, 1981.

McMillin, Harrison Crick, "High School Credit for Standardized Private Music Study in Kansas." Master's thesis, University of Chicago, 1916.

Meeks, Veronica. "A Historical Study of the Lawrence (Kansas) High School Orchestra, 1896-1953." Master's thesis, The University of Kansas, 1983.

Metcalf, Roy F. "Status of Music in Four Year and Senior High Schools in Kansas." Master's thesis, Northwestern University, 1930.

Moeller, Marsha G. "The History of Vocal Music in the Shawnee Mission, Kansas, Public Schools." Master's thesis, The University of Kansas, 1983.

Oursler, Robert D. "A History of Public School Music in Kansas." Master's thesis, Northwestern University, 1954.

Pereau, Warren C. "Survey of Music Teachers and Curriculum in Kansas High Schools." Master's thesis Colorado State College of Education, Greeley, 1941.

Peterson, Milo. "A Survey of Summer Band Programs in Twelve Kansas Communities." Master's thesis, Kansas State Teachers College, 1954.

Rarick, Margaret. "Music Teaching in the Rural Schools of Four Kansas Counties." Master's thesis, Northwestern University, 1932.

Regier, Bernard. "Music in Junior Colleges Generally and More Specifically in Kansas." Master's thesis, The University of Michigan, 1940.

Sease, Waldo. "The 1940 District Music Festivals in Kansas." Master's thesis, Colorado State College of Education, Greeley, 1941.

Seymour, Harriet. "The Certification of Music Teachers in Kansas, 1860-1930." Master's thesis, The University of Kansas, 1930.

Stone, Helen W. "The History of Music Education in the Kansas Community Junior Colleges, 1917-1965." Ph.D. diss., The University of Kansas, 1981.

Suderman, David H. "The Music Program of Church-Controlled Liberal Arts College in Kansas." Ph.D. diss., George Peabody College for Teachers, 1948.

Velásquez, Vivian. "The Music of Kansas Chautauquas." *Kansas Music Review* 52 (September 1990): 10-11, 37-38.

Wagner, Lavern John. "The Humboldt, Kansas Town Band: Its Times and Its Music from 1866 to 1881." *The Journal of Band Research* 24 (Spring 1989): 1-11.

Walker, Kenneth R. "The History of Public School Music in Iola, Kansas." Master's thesis, The University of Kansas, 1984.

White, James R. "A Survey of Instrumental Music Instruction in Public Schools of Second Class Cities of Kansas." Master's thesis, Kansas State Teachers College, Emporia, 1954.

Williams, Larry P. "A History of the High School Orchestra Movement in Kansas." Master's thesis, The University of Kansas, 1968.

Missouri

Cormier, Richard E. "The Founding of the St. Joseph Symphony Orchestra and Its Effects on School and Community: A Project in Community Music Education." Ed.D. diss., Columbia University, 1964.

Crabb, J. Milford. "A History of Music in Kansas City, 1900-1965." D.M.A. diss., University of Missouri, Kansas City, 1967.

Fly, Fenton C. "A History of Secondary Instrumental Music in the Public Schools of Kansas City, Missouri." D.M.A. diss., University of Missouri, Kansas City, 1967.

Justice, Delores Roberts. "The Early History of the Aesthetic Education Program at Central Midwestern Regional Educational Laboratory." Ed.D. diss., University of Illinois, 1988.

New Mexico

White, John E. "A Survey of the Organization and Administration of School Bands in New Mexico." Master's thesis, Texas Technical College, 1940.

Oklahoma

Adams, Kermit G. "Music in the Oklahoma Territory: 1889-1907." Ph.D. diss., North Texas State University, 1979.

Anderson, Edison H. "The Historical Development of Music in the Negro Secondary Schools of Oklahoma and at Langston University." Ph.D. diss., University of Iowa, 1957.

Cesario, Robert J. "An Investigation of the Original Works for Band Premiered at the Tri-State Music Festival in Enid, Oklahoma, 1934-1984." D.A. diss., University of Northern Colorado, 1990.

Fonder, Mark. Review of "A History of Instrumental Music in the Public Schools of Oklahoma Through 1945" (Ph.D. diss., The University of Oklahoma, 1989), by George H. McDow. *Bulletin of the Council for Research in Music Education* 110 (Fall 1991): 77-81.

Heller, George N. Review of "Music in the Oklahoma Territory: 1889-1907" (Ph.D. diss., North Texas State University, 1979), by Kermit G. Adams. In *Bulletin of the Council for Research in Music Education* 74 (Spring 1983): 72-75.

McDow, George H. "A History of Instrumental Music in the Public Schools of Oklahoma Through 1945." Ph.D. diss., The University of Oklahoma, 1989.

Watson, Charles J. "A Study of the Music Education Program of Southwestern State College, Weatherford, Oklahoma." Ed.D. diss., Columbia University, 1963.

Texas

Albrecht, Theodore J. "German Singing Societies in Texas." Ph.D. diss., North Texas State University, 1975.

Bakkegard, Benjamin M. "A History of Music Education in Texas." *Journal of Research in Music Education* 5 (Spring 1957): 36-45.

_____. Review of "Colonel Earl D. Irons: His Role in the History of Music Education in the Southwest to 1958" (Ph.D. diss., North Texas State University, 1982), by Gary Wayne Barlow. *Bulletin of the Council of Research in Music Education Bulletin* 76 (Fall 1983): 65-67.

Barrow, Gary W. "Colonel Earl D. Irons and the Early Development of Texas Bands." *The Journal of Band Research* 21 (Fall 1985): 9-30.

Bartley, Ruby Ruth. "A Brief Survey of the Historical Background and of the Present Status of Music Education in the Negro Schools of Texas." Master's thesis, Southwest Texas State University, 1950.

Biffle, George L. "A History of the Texas Music Educators Association, 1959-1979." D.M.A. diss., Arizona State University, 1991.

Brown, Lilla Jean. "Music in the History of Dallas, Texas, 1841-1900." Master's thesis, University of Texas, 1953.

Dabney, Ray F. "The History of the Band at Sam Houston State Teachers College." Master's thesis, Sam Houston State College, 1963.

Day, Robert L. "The Development of Music and Music Education in Ector County." Master's thesis, Hardin-Simmons University, 1956.

Edwin, George S. "Music and Music Education in Abilene, Texas: 1881-1911." Ph.D. diss., North Texas State University, 1983.

Eskridge, Charles S. "History of the Texas Music Educators Association." Master's thesis, Texas Technical College, 1943.

Foster, Mrs. Henry A. "A Study of the Development of Music in Hall County, Texas." Master's thesis, Hardin-Simmons University, 1942.

Grant, Daniel R. "The Texas Music Educators Association: A Historical Study of Selected Landmark Events Between 1938 and 1980 and the Decisions Which Influenced Their Outcomes." Ph.D. diss., University of North Texas, 1989.

Hackney, Charles R. "History of Texas Music Educators Association." Master's thesis, Sam Houston State Teachers College, 1939.

Harper, Minnie. "The Development of Music in the Curriculum of the Fort Worth Public Schools." Master's thesis, Texas Christian University, 1948.

Hughes, Olga I. "The Development of Music in the Amarillo Schools, 1889-1942." Master's thesis, Texas Technical College, 1942.

Jackson, Jo Anne. "The Organization and Development of String Programs in the Public Schools of Texas." Master's thesis, Baylor University, 1948.

Johnson, Roy J. "Music Education in Texas Higher Education Institutions, 1840-1947." Ed.D. diss., University of Texas, 1951.

Looser, Donald W. "Significant Factors in the Musical Development of the Cultural Life in Houston, Texas, 1930-1971." Ph.D. diss., The Florida State University, 1972.

Lopez, Elmo. "The History and Development of Music Education in Laredo, Texas." Master's thesis, University of Texas, 1957.

Martin, William. "The Texas Association of Music Schools: Its History and Curricular Function." Ed.D. diss., George Peabody College for Teachers of Vanderbilt University, 1956.

McGilvray, Byron W. "A Brief History of the Development of Music in Fort Worth, Texas, 1848-1972." Master's thesis, Texas Christian University, 1972.

McNeely, Lois T. "A History of Music Education in Wiley College." Master's thesis, University of Iowa, 1942.

Miles, Dorothy W. "A History of the School of Music of Baylor University." Master's thesis, Baylor University, 1950.

Miller, "The North Texas State University Jazz Degree: A History and Study of Its Significance." Ph.D. diss., Michigan State University, 1979.

Moore, Katrina L. "The History of the Development of Public School Music in Taylor County, Texas." Master's thesis,. North Texas State University, 1943.

Pefley, Wallace B. "The Evolution of Music Activities at Panola College, Carthage, Texas." Ed.D. diss., Columbia University, 1959.

Priest, Jimmie R. "A History of the West Texas State University Music Department, 1917-1965." Master's thesis, West Texas State University, 1965.

Pugh, Donald W. "Music in Frontier Houston, 1836-1876." D.M.A. diss., The University of Texas, 1970.

Sloan, David W. "History of Texas Public School Music." D.M.A. diss., The University of Texas, 1970.

Sowell, Brady O. "A History of the Texas Music Educators Association, 1940-1953." Master's thesis, Sam Houston State University, 1953.

Theriot, Leon R. "A History of the Texas Music Educators Association, 1953-1959." Master's thesis, Sam Houston State College, 1959.

Ware, Mary Anne. "Forty Years of Music in the Lubbock Public Schools (1900-1940)." Master's thesis, Texas Technical College, 1941.

Williams, Michael D. "A Historical Survey of Shape-Note Music and Practices in Texas." Master's thesis, University of Texas, 1970.

Worthington, Thomas H. "A History of the Development of Music Education in Austin, Texas." Master's thesis, University of Texas, 1954.

Young, Frances E. "Development of Public School Music in Sam Houston State Teachers College and Texas Technical College." Master's thesis, Texas Technical College, 1939.

Western Division

Timmerman, Maurine. "A History of the Western Division of the Music Educators National Conference." Ed.D. diss., University of Southern California, 1960.

Arizona

Ackerly, Julian M. "Tucson Arizona Boys Chorus: A History." Mus.D. diss., The University of Arizona, 1983.

Bakkegard, Benjamin M. "Music in Arizona Before 1912." *Journal of Research in Music Education* 8 (Fall 1960): 67-74.

Cordeiro, Joseph. "A Century of Musical Development in Tucson, Arizona, 1867-1967." A.Mus.D. diss., University of Arizona, 1968.

California

Baxter, Francis H. "A History of Music Education in the Los Angeles City Schools." D.Mus.A. diss, University of Southern California, 1960.

Cather, George D. "The Trend of Research Studies in Music Education at the University of Southern California, 1924-1949." Master's thesis, University of Southern California, 1950.

Choate, Robert A. "Music Instruction and Supervision in the Oakland Public Schools from 1868-1950." Ed.D. diss., Stanford University, 1950.

Del Monaco, John. "A History of the Bands of the University of Southern California, 1880-1952." Master's thesis, University of Southern California, 1952.

Fowells, Robert M. "A History of Music Education in the San Francisco Public Schools." D.Mus.A. diss., University of Southern California, 1959.

_____. "Public School Music in San Francisco, 1848 1897." *Journal of Research in Music Education* 11 (Spring 1963): 63-74.

Kjosness, Valborg. "Music at Stanford: The Development of Music Curricula in a University." Master's thesis, Stanford University, 1946.

Lindgren, Frank E. "A Content Analysis of Research Studies in Vocal Music Education at the University of Southern California from 1930-1955, with a View of Establishing Areas of Needful Research." Master's thesis, University of Southern California, 1956.

Schaub, David B. "A History of Public School Music Education in California: 1900-1955." Ph.D. diss., University of Southern California, 1960.

Wilson, Bruce D. "Implications of the Pillsbury Foundation School of Santa Barbara in Perspective." *Bulletin of the Council for Research in Music Education Bulletin* 68 (Fall 1981): 13-25.

Wilson, Neil E. "A History of Opera and Associated Education Activities in Los Angeles." Ph.D. diss., Indiana University, 1967.

Hawaii

Nevada

Utah

Garner, Ronald L. "A History of Music Education in the Granite School District of Salt Lake City, Utah." Ed.D. diss., University of Oregon, 1963.

Canada

Berg, Wesley P. "Choral Festivals and Choral Workshops Among the Mennonites of Manitoba and Saskatchewan, 1900-19650 with an Account of Early Developments in Russia." Ph.D. diss., University of Washington, 1979.

Brault, Diana V. "A History of the Ontario Music Educators' Association (1919-1974)." Ph.D. diss., The Eastman School of Music, University of Rochester, 1977.

Elliott, David J. "Jazz Education in Canada: Origins and Development." *The Bulletin of Historical Research in Music Education* 6 (January 1985): 17-28.

Green, F. Paul, and Nancy F. Vogan. *Education in Canada: A Historical Account*. Toronto: University of Toronto Press, 1991.

Heller, George N. Review of "A History of the Ontario Music Educators Association" (Ph.D. diss., The University of Rochester, Eastman School of Music, 1977), by Diana Victoria Brault. In *Bulletin of the Council for Research in Music Education* 68 (Fall 1981): 48-50.

Howell, Gordon P. "The Development of Music in Canada." Ph.D. diss., University of Rochester, 1959.

Lock, William R. "Ontario Church Choirs and Choral Societies, 1819-1918." D.M.A. diss., University of Southern California, 1972.

Trowsdale, G. C. "A History of Public School Music in Ontario." Ph.D. diss., University of Toronto, 1962.

Vogan, Nancy F. "The History of Public School Music in the Province of New Brunswick, 1872-1939." Ph.D. diss., The Eastman School of Music, University of Rochester, 1979.

Central and South America

Mexico

Heller, George N. "Music Education in the Valley of Mexico During the Sixteenth Century." Ph.D. diss., The University of Michigan, 1973.

Puerto Rico

Fitzmaurice, Robert M. "Music Education in Puerto Rico: A Historical Survey with Guidelines for an Exemplary Curriculum." Ph.D. diss, The Florida State University, 1970.

Europe

Breed, Victor T. "The Early Scholae Cantorum: From the Sixth to the Tenth Centuries." Master's thesis, The Catholic University of America, 1930.

Carpenter, Nan Cooke. *Music in Medieval and Renaissance Universities.* Norman, OK: The University of Oklahoma Press, 1958.

Wucher, Diethard. "Tenth Anniversary of the European Union of Music Schools (EMU)." *International Journal of Music Education* 3 (May 1984): 59-60.

Ireland

McCarthy, Marie F. "Music Education and the Quest for Cultural Identity in Ireland, 1831-1989." Ph.D. diss., The University of Michigan, 1990.

Germany

Livingstone, Ernest F. "The Place of Music in German Education from the Beginnings through the Sixteenth Century." *Journal of Research in Music Education* 15 (Winter 1967): 243-277.

Moeller, Lynn E. "Music in Germany During the Third Reich: The Use of Music for Propaganda." *Music Educators Journal* 67 (November 1980): 40-44.

Switzerland

Cecil, Leonard. "Switzerland: The Largest Country in the World." *The Quarterly* 1 (Winter 1990): 54-65.

Jarjisian, Catherine. Review of "An Historical and Philosophical Inquiry into the Development of Dalcroze Eurhythmics and Its Influence on Music Education in the French Cantons of Switzerland," by Linda Kyle Revkin (Ph.D. diss., Northwestern University, 1984). *Council for Research in Music Education Bulletin* 94 (Fall 1987): 37-41.

Revkin, Linda K. "An Historical and Philosophical Inquiry into the Development of Dalcroze Eurhythmics and Its Influence on Music Education in the French Cantons of Switzerland." Ph.D. diss., Northwestern University, 1984.

USSR

Pritzker, Maya. "The Music Education System in the USSR." *American Music Teacher* 41 (August-September 1991): 18-20, 62-64.

Remeta, Daniel R. "Music Education in the USSR." D.M.A. diss., University of Southern California, 1974.

United Kingdom

Allen, Elizabeth L. "Tonic Sol-Fa: Its Role in Nineteenth-Century Music Literacy in the United Kingdom." Ed.D. diss., University of Alabama, 1989.

Bagnall, Anne D. "Musical Practices in Medieval English Nunneries." Ph.D. diss., Columbia University, 1975.

Carpenter, Nan Cooke. "The Study of Music at the University of Oxford in the Middle Ages (to 1450)." *Journal of Research in Music Education* 1 (Spring 1953): 11-20.

Deverich, Robin K. "The Maidstone Movement: Influential Precursor of American Public School Instrumental Classes." *Journal of Research in Music Education* 35 (Spring 1987): 39-55.

Dobbs, Jack. "Music for a Small Planet at Dartington College of Arts." *International Journal of Music Education* 4 (November 1984): 15-20.

Mamminga, Michael. "British Brass Bands." *Music Educators Journal* 58 (November 1971): 82-83.

Owen, John. "Britten-Pears School for Advanced Musical Studies." *International Journal of Music Education* 3 (May 1984): 53-55.

Rainbow, Bernarr. *The Land Without Music: Musical Education in England 1800-1860*. Reprint ed. Aberystwyth, Dyfed, Wales: Boethius Press, 1990.

_____. *Music and the English Public School*. Aberystwyth, Dyfed, Wales: Boethius Press, 1990.

_____. *Music in Educational Thought and Practice: A Survey from 800 BC*. Aberystwyth, Dyfed, Wales: Boethius Press, 1990.

_____. *Some Notable Music Manuals*. Aberystwyth, Dyfed, Wales: Boethius Press, 1990.

Swing, Pamela S. "Fiddle Teaching in Shetland Isles Schools, 1973-1985." Ph.D. diss., The University of Texas at Austin, 1991.

Africa

Nigeria

Lo-Bamijoko, Joy Nwosu. "Music Education in Nigeria: The Status of Music Learning and Teaching." *The Quarterly* 1 (Winter 1990): 38-42.

Okafor, Richard C. "Music in Nigerian Education." *Bulletin of the Council for Research in Music Education* 108 (Spring 1991): 59-68.

South Africa

Oehrle, Elizabeth. "Music Education in South Africa." *The Quarterly* 1 (Winter 1990): 5-9.

Asia

Campbell, Patricia Shehan. Review of "Applications and Adaptations of Orff-Schulwerk in Japan, Taiwan, and Thailand" (Ph.D. diss., University of California, Los Angeles, 1988), by Mary Elizabeth Shamrock. *Bulletin of the Council for Research in Music Education* 108 (Spring 1991): 81-85.

China

Chung, Mai-lien. "The History and Use of Music in Chinese Christian Schools." Master's thesis, Boston University, 1923.

Japan

Kitayama, Atsuyasu. "Historical Changes in the Objectives of Japanese Music Education." *The Quarterly* 1 (Winter 1990): 32-37.

May, Elizabeth. "The Influence of the Meiji Period on Japanese Children's Music." *Journal of Research in Music Education* 13 (Summer 1965): 110-120.

_____. "Japanese Children's Music Before and After Contact with the West." Ph.D. diss., University of California, Los Angeles, 1958.

Ogawa, Masafumi. "American Contributions to the Beginning of Public Music Education in Japan." *The Bulletin of Historical Research in Music Education* 12 (July 1991): 113-128.

Korea

Kim, Anthony H. "The History of School Music Education in Korea from 1886 to the Present." Ed.D. diss., University of Northern Colorado, 1976.

Malaysia

Abdullah, Johami. "Music Education in Malaysia: An Overview." *The Quarterly* 1 (Winter 1990): 44-53.

Taiwan

Hsieh, Yuan-Mei. "The Status of Music Teaching and Learning in Taiwan." *The Quarterly* 1 (Winter 1990): 10-19.

Yik, Stephen Kai-Nin. "A Study of the Curriculum Materials Used in Music Classes in the Primary and Secondary Schools in Taiwan from 1950 to 1973." Ed.D. diss., Washington University, 1976.

Australia and the Pacific Islands

Kaeppler, Adrienne L. "Polynesian Music, Captain Cook, and the Romantic Movement in Europe." *Music Educators Journal* 65 (November 1978): 54-60.

Stevens, Robin S. "Music in State-Supported Education in New South Wales and Victoria, 1848-1920." Ph.D. diss., University of Melbourne, 1979.

III. OTHER

Books

Abeles, Harold, Charles R. Hoffer, and Robert H. Klotman. *Foundations of Music Education*. New York: Schirmer Books, 1984.

Arneson, Arne Jon. *The* Music Educators Journal*: Cumulative Index 1914-1987*. Stevens Point, WI: Index House, 1987.

Bentley, Arnold. *Music in Education: A Point of View*. Windsor, Berks, England: NFER Publishing Company, Ltd., 1975.

Birge, Edward Bailey. *History of Public School Music in the United States*. Boston: Oliver Ditson Company, 1928. Also available in a "New and Augmented edition," Bryn Mawr, PA: Oliver Ditson Company, 1937; and in a reprint of the 1937 edition, Washington, DC: Music Educators National Conference, 1966.

Brookhart, Edward. *Music in American Higher Education: An Annotated Bibliography*. Bibliographies in American Music, No. 10. Warren, MI: Harmonie Park Press, 1988.

Campbell, Patricia Shehan. *Lessons from the World: A Cross-Cultural Guide to Music Teaching and Learning*. New York: Schirmer Books, 1991.

Chase, Gilbert. *America's Music: From the Pilgrims to the Present*. 3rd ed. Urbana, IL: University of Illinois Press, 1987.

Cobb, Buell E., Jr. *The Sacred Harp: A Tradition and Its Music*. Athens, GA: University of Georgia Press, 1978. Reprint ed., 1989.

Egan, Robert F. *Music and the Arts in the Community: The Community Music School in America*. Metuchen, NJ: The Scarecrow Press, 1989.

Elson, Louis C. *The History of American Music*, 3rd ed. Revised by Arthur C. Elson. New York: Macmillan, 1925.

Gary, Charles L. *Vignettes of Music Education History*. Washington, DC: Music Educators National Conference, 1964.

Goodman, A. Harold. *Music Education: Perspectives and Perceptions*. Dubuque, IA: Kendall-Hunt Publishing Company, 1982.

Hamm, Charles. *Music in the New World*. New York: W. W. Norton and Company, 1983.

Hitchcock, H. Wiley. *Music in the United States: A Historical Introduction*. 3rd ed. Englewood Cliffs, NJ: Prentice-Hall, Inc., 1988.

Hitchcock, H. Wiley, and Stanley Sadie, Eds. *The New Grove Dictionary of American Music*, 4 vols. London: Macmillan Press Limited, 1986.

Howard, John Tasker. *Our American Music: Three Hundred Years of It*. 4th ed. New York: Thomas Y. Crowell Co., 1965.

Keene, James A. *A History of Music Education in the United States*. Hanover, NH: University Press of New England, 1982.

Kingman, Daniel L. *American Music: A Panorama*, 2nd ed. New York: Schirmer Books, 1990.

Lang, Paul Henry, ed. *One Hundred Years of Music in America*. New York: G. Schirmer, 1961.

Leonhard, Charles, and Robert W. House. *Foundations and Principles of Music Education*. 2nd ed. New York: McGraw-Hill Book Co., 1972.

Lowens, Irving. *Music and Musicians in Early America*. New York: W. W. Norton and Company, Inc., 1964.

Mark, Michael L. *Contemporary Music Education*. 2nd ed. New York: Schirmer Books, Inc., 1986.

_____. *Source Readings in Music Education History*. New York: Schirmer Books, 1982.

Mark, Michael L., and Charles L. Gary. *A History of American Music Education*. New York: Schirmer Books, 1991.

Phelps, Roger P. *A Guide to Research in Music Education*. 3rd ed. Metuchen, NJ: The Scarecrow Press, 1986.

Rainbow, Edward L., and Hildegard C., Froelich. *Research in Music Education: An Introduction to Systematic Inquiry*. New York: Schirmer Books, 1987.

Ritter, Frédéric Louis, *Music in America*, 2nd ed. New York Scribner and Sons, 1890.

Sonneck, Oscar, G. T. *Suum Cuique: Essays in Music*. New York: G. Schirmer, 1916.

Southern, Eileen. *The Music of Black Americans: A History*. 2nd ed. New York: W. W., Norton and Company, 1983.

Sunderman, Lloyd F. *Historical Foundations of Music Education in the United States*. Metuchen, NJ: The Scarecrow Press, 1971.

Tellstrom, A. Theodore. *Music in American Education: Past and Present*. New York: Holt, Rinehart and Winston, Inc., 1971.

Ulrich, Homer. *A Centennial History of the Music Teachers National Association*. Cincinnati, OH: Music Teachers National Association, Inc., 1976.

Book Chapters, Periodicals, Yearbooks, and Proceedings

Allen, Michael L. "Have You Ever Wondered Where the First Public School Orchestra Began?" *Update* 3 (Fall 1984): 26-28.

Alper, Clifford D. "The Early Childhood Song Books of Eleanor Smith: Their Affinity with the Philosophy of Friedrich Froebel." *Journal of Research in Music Education* 28 (Summer 1980): 111-118.

_____. "Froebelian Implications in Texts of Early Childhood Songs Published Near the Turn of the Century." *Journal of Research in Music Education* 30 (Spring 1982): 49-60.

_____. "Instinct and Imagination: Froebel's Principle of Self-Activity in Turn-of-the-Century Songbooks." *Music Educators Journal* 72 (October 1985): 53-63.

"America's Momentous Contribution to Public School Music." *Etude* 50 (April 1932): 237.

Aquino, John. "A Gallery of Early MENC Conferences." *Music Educators Journal* 65 (March 1979): 62-67.

Baldwin, Ralph R. "From the Civil War to 1900: Settling the Problem of Reading." *MTNA Proceedings* (1922): 166-179.

Ball, Charles H. "CMP: A Personal View." *The Quarterly* 1 (Autumn 1990): 61-63.

Barnes, Stephen H. "The Sociology of Music Education: Conceptual Foundations and Historical Referents." *Contributions to Music Education* 8 (1980): 93-95.

Barresi, Anthony L. "The Role of the Federal Government in Support of the Arts and Music Education." *Journal of Research in Music Education* 29 (Winter 1981): 245-256.

Bennett, Don. "CM in Memphis: Evolution of a Revolution." *The Quarterly* 1 (Autumn 1990): 55-57.

Bennett, Peggy. "From Hungary to America: The Evolution of Education Through Music." *Music Educators Journal* 74 (September 1987): 36-45, 60.

Bergee, Martin J. "Ringing the Changes: General John Eaton and the 1886 Public School Music Survey." *Journal of Research in Music Education* 35 (Summer 1987): 103-116.

Bicknell, Thomas W. "Music in Public Education." *MTNA Proceedings* (1885): 176-189.

Birge, Edward Bailey. "Music Appreciation: The Education of the Listener." *MTNA Proceedings* (1922): 189-193.

_____. "One Hundred Years of School Music." *Music Educators Journal* 22 (September 1935): 19.

_____. "Public School Music, 1838-1938." *Music Educators Journal* 24 (February 1938): 13-14.

"Black Musicians Leading the Way." *Music Educators Journal* 68 (February 1982): 46-48.

Blum, Beula Eisenstadt. "Solmization and Pitch Notation in Nineteenth-Century American School Music Textbooks." *Journal of Research in Music Education* 19 (Winter 1971): 443-552.

Boyer, Horace Clarence. "Gospel Music." *Music Educators Journal* 64 (May 1987): 34-43.

Brandt, Thompson A. "Summer Music Camps: A Historical Perspective." *The Bulletin of Historical Research in Music Education* 9 (July 1988): 119-130.

Breckenridge, Rose Trahey. "History and Culture in the Study of Works of Art: The Question of Aesthetic Relevance." *Contributions to Music Education* 8 (1980): 55-72.

Britton, Allen P. "Founding *JRME*: A Personal View." *Journal of Research in Music Education* 32 (Winter 1984): 233-242.

_____. "The How and Why of Teaching Singing Schools in Eighteenth-Century America." *Bulletin of the Council for Research in Music Education* 99 (Winter 1989): 7-22.

_____. "Keokuk to San Antonio: 75 Years of Change." *Music Educators Journal* 68 (February 1982): 42-44.

_____. "Music Education: An American Specialty." In *Perspectives in Music Education: Source Book III*, pp. 15-28. Edited by Bonnie C. Kowall. Washington, DC: Music Educators National Conference, 1966.

_____. "Music in Early American Public Education: A Historical Critique." In *Basic Concepts in Music Education*, pp. 195-211. Edited by Nelson B. Henry. Chicago: National Society for the Study of Education, 1958.

_____. "Musical Education in the United States of America." *The Bulletin of Historical Research in Music Education* 3 (July 1982): 91-102.

_____. "The Place of Historical Research in Graduate Programs in Music Education." *The Bulletin of Historical Research in Music Education* 5 (July 1984): 55-57.

_____. "Research in the United States." *Journal of Research in Music Education* 17 (Spring 1969): 108-111.

Brook, Barry S. "Oral History and Music in Our Time." *College Music Symposium* 19 (Spring 1979): 233-238.

Burton, Leon. "Comprehensive Musicianship—The Hawaii Curriculum Project." *The Quarterly* 1 (Autumn 1990): 67-76.

Callaway, Frank. "ISME—The First Twenty-Five Years." *College Music Symposium* 19 (Spring 1979): 239-242.

Campbell, Patricia Shehan. "Rhythmic Movement and Public School Music Education: Conservative and Progressive Views of the Formative Years." *Journal of Research in Music Education* 39 (Spring 1991): 12-22.

Caylor, Florence. "On the Trendmill of Elementary Music Education." *Music Educators Journal* 58 (March 1972): 33-37.

Chernin, Mallorie. "A Practical Application of an Eighteenth-Century Aesthetic: The Development of Pestalozzian Education." *College Music Symposium* 26 (1986): 53-65.

Clark, Frances Elliott. "School Music in 1836, 1886, 1911, and 1936." *NEA Proceedings* (1924): 603-611.

Clark, Jessie L. "Some Musical History." *School Music Monthly* 7 (November 1906): 21-22.

Coburn, E. L. "Music in the United States for the Last Twenty-Five Years." *MSNC Proceedings* (1910): 16-19.

Coffman, Don D. "Vocal Music and the Classroom Teacher, 1885 to 1905." *Journal of Research in Music Education* 35 (Summer 1987): 92-102.

Copeland, Robert M. "Music Historiography in the Classroom." *College Music Symposium* 19 (Spring 1979): 140-155.

Crawford, Richard. "Musical Learning in Nineteenth-Century America." *American Music* 1 (Spring 1983): 1-11.

Damrosch, Frank. "Music in the Public Schools." In *The American History and Encyclopedia of Music*, Vol. 7, pp. 17-37. Edited by W. L. Hubbard. New York: Irving Square, 1908.

Dickey, Frances M. "The Early History of Public School Music in the United States." *MTNA Proceedings* (1913): 185-209. See also, *School Music* 15 (May 1914): 5-16, 19-23.

Diemer, Emma Lou. "A Composer in the Schools." *The Quarterly* 1 (Autumn 1990): 33-34.

Doane, Christopher P. "A Brief History of Instrumental Music Education in the United States." *Update* 4 (Fall 1985): 15-19.

Douglas, Charles Winfred. "The History and Work of the Schola Cantorum." *MTNA Proceedings* (1913): 248-260.

Eaklor, Vicki L. "Roots of an Ambivalent Culture: Music, Education, and Music Education in Antebellum America." *Journal of Research in Music Education* 33 (Summer 1985): 87-89.

Earhart, Will. "The Evolution of High School Music." *MTNA Proceedings* (1922): 184-188.

Eaton, John. "Education in Music at Home and Abroad." *MTNA Proceedings* (1885): 51-68.

Eddins, John. "A Brief History of Computer-Assisted Instruction in Music." *College Music Symposium* 21 (Fall 1981): 7-14.

Eddy, M. Alexandra. "American Violin Method-Books and European Teachers, Geminiani to Spohr." *American Music* 8 (Summer 1990): 167-209.

Efland, Arthur. "Art and Music in the Pestalozzian Tradition." *Journal of Research in Music Education* 31 (Fall 1983): 165-178.

Elward, Thomas J. "They Made Black History." *Music Educators Journal* 67 (February 1981): 35-38.

Eskew, Harry. "Southern Harmony and Its Era." *The Hymn* 41 (October 1990): 28-39.

Folstrom, Roger J. "History of Composers in the Schools Project." *Music Educators Journal* 70 (September 1983): 63.

Fonder, Mark. "Band Lessons by Mail: A Look at Musical Correspondence Schools of the Early Twentieth Century." *The Bulletin of Historical Research in Music Education* 13 (January 1992): 1-7.

_____. "Discover Your Band or Orchestra's Roots." *Music Educators Journal* 77 (September 1990): 40-45.

Foy, Patricia S. "A Brief Look at the Community Song Movement." *Music Educators Journal* 76 (January 1990): 26-27.

Fromme, Arnold. "Performance Technique on Brass Instruments During the Seventeenth Century." *Journal of Research in Music Education* 20 (Fall 1972): 329-343.

"The Founding of MENC: Reprints from *School Music Monthly*." *The Bulletin of Historical Research in Music Education* 3 (January 1982): 1-18.

Fouts, Gordon E. "Music Instruction in Early Nineteenth-Century American Monitorial Schools." *Journal of Research in Music Education* 22 (Summer 1974): 112-119.

_____. "Music in the Education of American Youth: The Early Academies." *Journal of Research in Music Education* 20 (Winter 1972): 469-476.

Gary, Charles L. "A Tradition of Progress: Seventy-Five Years of *MEJ*." *Music Educators Journal* 76 (April 1990): 53-58.

Gates, J. Terry. "A Comparison of the Tune Books of Tufts and Walters." *Journal of Research in Music Education* 36 (Fall 1988): 169-193.

_____. "*Fermez la port?*: On Michael L. Mark's 'A New Look at Historical Periods in American Music Education.'" *Bulletin of the Council for Research in Music Education Bulletin* 103 (Winter 1990): 29-34.

_____. "A Historical Comparison of Public Singing by American Men and Women." *Journal of Research in Music Education* 37 (Spring 1989): 32-37.

Gehrkens, Karl W. "Origin and Growth of Music Education in America." *Musical America* 59 (September 1959): 25-44.

_____. " The Twentieth Century—A Singing Revival." *MTNA Proceedings* (1922): 179-184.

Gfeller, Kate, and Alice-Ann Darrow. "Ten Years of Mainstreaming: Where Are We Now?" *Music Educators Journal* 74 (October 1987): 27-30.

Gonzo, Carroll. "Aesthetic Experience: A Coming of Age in Music Education." *Music Educators Journal* 58 (December 1971): 34-37.

_____. "On Writing a Critical Review." *Council for Research in Music Education Bulletin* 28 (Spring 1972): 14-22.

Gordon, Edgar B. "The Birth of School Bands and Orchestras." *Music Educators Journal* 43 (November-December 1956): 34-36, 43-45.

Gordon, Edwin E. "Sequencing Music Skills and Content." *American Music Teacher* 41 (October-November 1991): 22-23, 48-51.

Gordon, Roderick Dean. "Research in Music Education." In *Music Education in Action: Basic Principles and Practical Methods*, pp. 366-376. Edited by Archie N. Jones. Boston: Allyn and Bacon, Inc., 1960.

Grashel, John W. "An Analysis of Giorgio Antoniotto's *L'Arte armonica; or, A Treatise on the Composition of Musick*." *The Bulletin of Historical Research in Music Education* 7 (January 1986): 13-21.

_____. "The Gamut and Solmization in Early British and American Texts." *Journal of Research in Music Education* 29 (Spring 1981): 63-70.

Gray, Sharon L. "An Overview of the Historical Development of Catholic Music Education in the United States." *The Bulletin of Historical Research in Music Education* 12 (January 1991): 27-49.

Guion, David M. "From Yankee Doodle Thro' to Handel's Largo: Music at the World's Columbian Exposition." *College Music Symposium* 24 (Spring 1984): 81-96.

Haack, Paul A. "An Analysis of the Values Expressed in the Song Texts of an 1873 Music Education Book." *The Bulletin of Historical Research in Music Education* 4 (January 1983): 7-13.

Hall, Harry H. "Moravian Music Education in America, ca. 1750 to ca. 1830." *Journal of Research in Music Education* 29 (Fall 1981): 225-234.

Heller, George N. "Art, Science, and Pedagogy: Music Education in America in the Nineties." *Update* 2 (Summer 1984): 24-25.

_____. "Celebrate the Sesquicentennial!" *Music Educators Journal* 74 (September 1987): 28-31.

_____. "Discipline and Music Education: Some Historical Considerations." *Update* 1 (Fall 1982): 23-25.

_____. "Discipline and Recreation: Music Education in the Eighties." *Update* 2 (Fall 1983): 21-22.

_____. "A Historical View of Research in Music Education." *Update* 1 (May 1982): 25-26.

_____. "Listening Activities in Music Education: Some Exemplars from Historical Research." *Update* 8 (Fall-Winter 1989): 3-8.

_____. "Methods in Teaching Music: Toward (Yet) Another Centennial." *Update* 1 (Spring 1983): 25-27.

_____. "Music Contests and Festivals: Some Ethno-Historical Considerations." *Update* 3 (Fall 1984): 23-24.

_____. "Music Education History: A Short, Selective Bibliography." *Music Educators Journal* 74 (December 1987): 24-25.

_____. "On the Meaning and Value of Historical Research in Music Education." *Journal of Research in Music Education* 33 (Spring 1985): 4-6.

_____. "Retrospective of Multicultural Music Education in the United States." *Music Educators Journal* 69 (May 1983): 35-36.

_____. "Setting Sights on Our Centennial." *Music Educators Journal* 68 (May 1982): 29.

_____. "The Society for Research in Music Education: A Brief Historical Perspective." *Update* 5 (Summer 1987): 15-16.

Heller, George N., and Rudolf E. Radocy. "On the Significance of Significance: Addressing a Basic Problem in Research." *Bulletin of the Council for Research in Music Education* 73 (Winter 1983): 50-58.

Heller, George N., and Bruce D. Wilson. "Historical Research in Music Education: A Prolegomenon." *Bulletin of the Council for Research in Music Education Bulletin* 69 (Winter 1982): 1-20.

Hilton, Lewis B. "For the Insomniac Music Education Historian." *The Bulletin of Historical Research in Music Education* 2 (July 1981): 35-38.

Hinely, Mary Brown. "The Uphill Climb of Women in American Music: Part I—Performers and Teachers." *Music Educators Journal* 70 (April 1984): 31-35.

Holt, Hosea E. "Music in Public Schools." *Education* 4 (January 1884): 262-270.

Holz, Emil A. "The National School Band Tournament of 1923 and Its Bands." *The Journal of Band Research* 2 (Autumn 1966): 17-21.

_____. "The Schools Band Contest of America (1923)." *Journal of Research in Music Education* 10 (Spring 1962): 3-12.

Hood, Marguerite V. "Index of Yearbooks of the Music Educators National Conference, 1925-1938." *MENC Proceedings* (1939-1940): 512-552.

Humphreys, Jere T. "Applications of Science: The Age of Standardization and Efficiency in Music Education." *The Bulletin of Historical Research in Music Education* 9 (January 1988): 1-21.

_____. "The Child-Study Movement and Public School Music Education." *Journal of Research in Music Education* 33 (Summer 1985): 79-86.

_____. "Music Eduction and the School-Survey Movement." *The Bulletin of Historical Research in Music Education* 8 (January 1987): 33-44.

_____. "An Overview of American Public School Bands and Orchestras Before World War II." *Bulletin of the Council for Research in Music Education* 101 (Summer 1989): 50-60.

_____. "Periodical Literature in Music Education: A Historical Overview." *Update* 3 (Summer 1985): 18-19.

_____. "Strike Up the Band! The Legacy of Patrick S. Gilmore." *Music Educators Journal* 74 (October 1987): 22-26.

_____. "Theory Versus Performance in Music Education." *Update* 5 (Fall 1986): 15-17.

Hunter, Leslie L. "The Role of Music in the 1840 Campaign of William Henry Harrison." *The Bulletin of Historical Research in Music Education* 10 (July 1989): 107-110.

Hylton, John. "A Survey of Choral Education Research: 1972-1982." *Bulletin of the Council for Research in Music Education* 76 (Fall 1983): 1-29.

Jansky, Nelson M. "On the Top Floor of the Old Pope Cycle Building." *Music Educators Journal* 60 (September 1973): 50-54.

Jepson, Benjamin. "The Science of Music vs. Rote Practice in Public Schools." *MTNA Proceedings* (1887): 174-187.

John, Robert W. "Nineteenth Century Graded Vocal Series." *Journal of Research in Music Education* 2 (Fall 1954): 103-118.

_____. "Origins of the First Music Educators Convention." *Journal of Research in Music Education* 13 (Winter 1965): 207-219.

_____. "The Second Hundred Years." *Music Educators Journal* 51 (February-March 1965): 103-104.

Johnson, H. Earle. "Musical Interest of Certain American Literary and Political Figures." *Journal of Research in Music Education* 19 (Fall 1971): 272-294.

_____. "The Need for Research in the History of American Music." *Journal of Research in Music Education* 6 (Spring 1958): 43-61.

Julius, Ruth. "Oral History in Music: A Practical Guide." *College Music Symposium* 20 (Spring 1980): 96-104.

"Keokuk in 1907: More Reprints from *School Music Monthly*." *The Bulletin of Historical Research in Music Education* 3 (July 1982): 51-90.

Klein, Nancy Kirkland. "Music and Music Education in the Shaker Societies of America." *The Bulletin of Historical Research in Music Education* 11 (January 1990): 33-47.

Koch, Franklin. "Cooperative Promotional Efforts of the Music Supervisors National Conference and the National Bureau for the Advancement of Music." *Journal of Research in Music Education* 38 (Winter 1990): 269-281.

Kolman, Barry H. "Early American Wind Music in General Instrumental Tutors, 1800-1836," *The Journal of Band Research* 23 (Fall 1987): 61-77.

Koza, Julia Eklund. "Music Instruction in the Nineteenth Century: Views from *Godey's Lady's Book*, 1830-77." *Journal of Research in Music Education* 38 (Winter 1990): 245-257.

Kraft, Ivor. "Music for the Feeble-Minded in Nineteenth-Century America." *Journal of Research in Music Education* 11 (Fall 1963): 119-122.

Kresteff, Assen D. "Musica Disciplina and Musica Sonora." *Journal of Research in Music Education* 10 (Spring 1962): 13-29.

Lawrence, Clara E. "Early School Music Methods." *Music Educators Journal* 25 (December 1938): 20-22.

Leonhard, Charles. "Where's the Beef?" *The Bulletin of Historical Research in Music Education* 3 (July 1985): 58-60.

Levy, Alan Howard. "Music's Proper Place: Trends in the Status of Music at Selected Institutions of Higher Education in America, 1870-1920." *Bulletin of the Council for Research in Music Education* 72 (Fall 1982): 16-39.

Livingston, Carolyn. "Characteristics of American Women Composers: Implications for Music Education." *Update* 20 (Fall-Winter 1991): 15-18.

Lowens, Irving, and Allen P. Britton. "*The Easy Instructor* (1798-1831): A History and Bibliography of the First Shape Note Tune Book." *Journal of Research in Music Education* 1 (Spring 1953): 31-54.

Luty, Bryce. "Jazz Education's Struggle for Acceptance." *Music Educators Journal* 69 (November 1982): 38-39, 53.

_____. "Jazz Ensembles' Era of Accelerated Growth." *Music Educators Journal* 69 (December 1982): 49-50, 64.

"MEJ at 60." *Music Educators Journal* 61 (September 1974): 45-52.

Mailman, Martin. "CM: The Uncommon Elements." *The Quarterly* 1 (Autumn 1990): 35-38.

Mark, Michael L. "A New Look at Historical Periods in American Music Education." *Bulletin of the Council for Research in Music Education* 99 (Winter 1989): 1-6.

_____. "The Effect of Eclecticism on American Music Education." *The Bulletin of Historical Research in Music Education* 4 (July 1983): 33-38.

_____. "The Evolution of Music Education Philosophy from Utilitarian to Aesthetic." *Journal of Research in Music Education* 30 (Spring 1982): 15-21.

_____. "The Fragmentation of the Music Education Profession." *College Music Symposium* 21 (Spring 1981): 103-111.

_____. "The GO Project: Retrospective of a Decade." *Music Educators Journal* 67 (December 1980): 42-47.

_____. "In and Out of the Mainstream: History Repeats Itself with the School Jazz Band." *Music Educators Journal* 62 (November 1975): 62-67.

_____. "MENC and World War II Programs." *Music Educators Journal* 67 (November 1980): 44-47.

_____. "Music Education's Cultural Imperative." *Music Educators Journal* 74 (December 1987): 23-26.

_____. "The Music Educators National Conference and World War II Home Front Programs." *The Bulletin of Historical Research in Music Education* 1 (July 1980): 1-16.

_____, "A New Look at Historical Periods in American Music Education." *Bulletin of the Council for Research in Music Education* 99 (Winter 1989): 1-6.

_____. "Unique Aspects of Historical Research in Music Education." *The Bulletin of Historical Research in Music Education* 6 (January 1985): 29-34.

Mark, Michael L., and Ancell Patten. "The Emergence of the Modern Marching Band—1950 to 1970." *The Instrumentalist* (June 1976).

Mathis, William. "The Emergence of Simple Instrument Experiences in Early Kindergartens." *Journal of Research in Music Education* 20 (Summer 1972): 255-261.

_____. "Simple Instrument Experiences in School Music Programs from 1900." *Journal of Research in Music Education* 21 (Fall 1973): 270-275.

McCarrell, Lamar K. "The Impact of World War II upon the College Band." *The Journal of Band Research* 10 (Fall 1973): 3-8.

McConathy, Osbourne. "From Lowell Mason to the Civil War: A Period of Pioneers." *MTNA Proceedings* (1923): 158-166.

McManus, John C. "'Rats in the Attic' and other Musical Explorations." *The Quarterly* 1 (Autumn 1990): 51-54.

Miller, Samuel D. "The First Three National High School Choruses: Experiments in Excellence." *The Bulletin of Historical Research in Music Education* 5 (July 1984): 29-38.

_____. "Initial Reading Keys Exemplified in American Textbooks, 1875-1988." *The Bulletin of Historical Research in Music Education* 11 (January 1990): 1-16.

_____. "*The Music Hour* (1927-1941) and Its Pioneer Listening-Appreciation Program." *The Bulletin of Historical Research in Music Education* 12 (January 1991): 1-12.

_____. "Music, Education, Recent History, and Ideas." *Bulletin of the Council for Research in Music Education Bulletin* 77 (Winter 1984): 1-19.

_____. "Music Reading Programs Established in Selected General Music Textbooks of the 1940s." *The Bulletin of Historical Research in Music Education* 4 (July 1983): 25-32.

_____. "Pianos in the Classroom: A Historical Perspective." *Music Educators Journal* 74 (March 1988): 26-29.

_____. "Time, Space, and the Music Educator." *The Bulletin of Historical Research in Music Education* 13 (January 1992): 19-32.

Miller, Thomas W. "Comprehensive Musicianship at East Carolina University, 1966-1968." *The Quarterly* 1 (Autumn 1990): 58-60.

_____. "The Influence of Progressivism on Music Education, 1917-1947." *Journal of Research in Music Education* 14 (Spring 1966): 3-16.

Mitchell, Melvin. "Know Where to Look: Finding Early American Music for Performance." *Music Educators Journal* 62 (October 1975): 62-63.

Molnar, John W. "Changing Aspects of American Culture as Reflected in the MENC." *Journal of Research in Music Education* 7 (Fall 1959): 174-184.

_____. "The Establishment of the Music Supervisors National Conference, 1907-1910." *Journal of Research in Music Education* 3 (Spring 1955): 40-50.

_____. "The Organization and Development of the Sectional Conferences." *Journal of Research in Music Education* 1 (Fall 1953): 127-134.

Moore, James E. "National School Band Contests Between 1926 and 1931." *Journal of Research in Music Education* 20 (Summer 1972): 233-245.

"Musical Education." In *The American History and Encyclopedia of Music*, Vol. 7, pp. 173-203. Edited by W. L. Hubbard. New York: Irving Squire, 1908.

Nelson, Carl B., and David B. Williams. "Review and Survey of MENC Research Training Institutes." *Journal of Research in Music Education* 25 (Spring 1977): 3-20.

The New Grove Dictionary of Music and Musicians, 1980 ed. S.v. "Education in Music," by Richard J. Colwell.

The New Grove Dictionary of American Music, 1986 ed. S.v. "Education in Music," by Richard J. Colwell.

The New Harvard Dictionary of Music, 1986 ed. S.v. "Education in the United States."

The New Oxford Companion to Music, 1983 ed. S.v. "Education and Music," by Keith Stanwick.

Nolte, Eckhard. "Didactic Considerations of Music Teaching in Some Compendiums for Musical Instruction from A.D. 1600." *Bulletin of the Council for Research in Music Education Bulletin* 91 (Spring 1987): 138-142.

Olsen, Dale A. "Public Concerts in Early America." *Music Educators Journal* 65 (May 1979): 48-59.

Owen, Barbara. "The Bay Psalm Book and Its Era." *The Hymn* 41 (October 1990): 12-19.

Parthun, Paul. "Tribal Music in North America." *Music Educators Journal* 62 (January 1976): 32-45.

Pemberton, Carol A. "The *Manual of the Boston Academy of Music*, 1834: A Remarkable Book." *The Bulletin of Historical Research in Music Education* 7 (July 1986): 41-54.

_____. "The Past Is Prelude." *Music Educators Journal* 73 (May 1987): 37.

_____. "Revisionist Historians: Writers Reflected in Their Writings." *Journal of Research in Music Education* 35 (Winter 1987): 213-220.

_____. "'Singing Merrily, Merrily, Merrily': Songs for the Skeptics of 1838." *American Music* 6 (Spring 1988): 74-87.

Perkins, Henry S. "Reminiscences of Early Days in School Music." *School Music* 8 (May 1908): 5-9.

Perrin, Phil D. "Pedagogical Philosophy, Methods, and Materials of American Tune Book Introductions: 1801-1860." *Journal of Research in Music Education* 18 (Spring 1970): 65-69.

_____. "Systems of Scale Notation in Nineteenth-Century American Tune Books." *Journal of Research in Music Education* 18 (Fall 1970): 257-264.

Phelps, Roger P. "The First Earned Doctorate in Music Education." *The Bulletin of Historical Research in Music Education* 4 (January 1983): 1-6.

_____. "The Mendelssohn Quintet Club: A Milestone in American Music Education." *Journal of Research in Music Education* 8 (Spring 1960): 39-44.

Pincherle, Marc. "Elementary Musical Instruction in the Eighteenth Century." *Musical Quarterly* 34 (January 1948): 61-67.

Platt, Melvin C. "The History and Development of the American Institute of Normal Methods, 1914-1950." *Contributions to Music Education* 2 (1973): 31-39. See also, *A Cross-Section of Research in Music Education*, Stephen H. Barnes, ed., 248-258. Washington, DC: University Press of America, Inc., 1982.

Platt, Melvin C. and David S. McGuire. "The Incidence of History of Music Education Teaching: Report of a Survey." *The Bulletin of Historical Research in Music Education* 9 (January 1988): 23-60.

Pond, Donald. "A Composer's Study of Young Children's Innate Musicality." *Bulletin of the Council of Research in Music Education* 68 (Fall 1981): 1-12.

_____. "The Young Child's Playful World of Sound." *Music Educators Journal* 66 (March 1980): 38-41.

Porter, Lewis. "'She Wiped All the Men Out.'" *Music Educators Journal* 71 (September 1984): 43-52.

_____. "'You Can't Get There Timidly.'" *Music Educators Journal* 71 (October 1984): 42-51.

Pucciani, Donna. "Sexism in Music Education: Survey of the Literature, 1972-1982." *Music Educators Journal* 70 (September 1983): 49-51, 68-73.

Rice, Charles I. "Boston, the Cradle of Public-School Music in America." *MTNA Proceedings* (1910): 798-803; see also, *School Music* 11 (September 1910): 36-40.

Rideout, Roger R. "Music Education and the 'New History.'" *The Bulletin of Historical Research in Music Education* 8 (January 1987): 45-54.

Riley, Maurice. "A Tentative Bibliography of Early Wind Instrument Tutors." *Journal of Research in Music Education* 6 (Spring 1958): 3-24.

Roske, Michael. "The Professionalism of Private Music Teaching in the Nineteenth Century: A Study with Social Statistics." *Bulletin of the Council for Research in Music Education Bulletin* 91 (Spring 1987): 143-148.

Rutkowski, Joanne. "The Child Voice: An Historical Perspective." *The Bulletin of Historical Research in Music Education* 6 (January 1985): 1-16.

Scholten, James W. "Born in the U.S.A.: Vernacular Music and Public Education." *Music Educators Journal* 74 (January 1988): 22-25.

_____. "Historical Research in Music Education: A Case of Intentional Neglect." *Contributions to Music Education* 7 (1979): 64-67.

_____. "The Tunebook That Roars: The Sound and Style of Sacred Harp Singing." *Music Educators Journal* 66 (February 1980): 32-37.

Shetler, Donald J. "Past, A Museum—Present, Uncertain Signs—Future, Possible Progress." *Update* 1 (Fall 1982): 17-19.

Solomon, Alan L. "Music in Special Education Before 1930: Hearing and Speech Development." *Journal of Research in Music Education* 28 (Winter 1980): 236-242.

Standifer, James A. "Comprehensive Musicianship: A Multicultural Perspective—Looking Back to the Future." *The Quarterly* 1 (Autumn 1990): 10-19.

Stoddard, Hope E. "Early Colonists and the Bars-Vile." *Music Educators Journal* 67 (April 1981): 50-51.

Sunderman, Lloyd F. "The Era of Beginnings in American Music Education (1830-1840)." *Journal of Research in Music Education* 4 (Spring 1956): 33-39.

Terri, Salli. "The Gift of Shaker Music." *Music Educators Journal* 62 (September 1975): 22-35.

Thompson, William. "The Anatomy of a Flawed Success: Comprehensive Musicianship Revisited." *The Quarterly* 1 (Autumn 1990): 20-28.

Troth, Eugene W. "Changes and Challenges: Convention Patterns of the MENC." *Music Educators Journal* 67 (February 1981): 48-56.

_____. "An Executive Secretary for the Music Educators National Conference: A Process of Organizational Change." *The Bulletin of Historical Research in Music Education* 2 (January 1981): 3-9.

_____. "What's in a Name?" *Music Educators Journal* 68 (February 1982): 44-45.

Turrentine, Edgar M. "Historical Research in Music Education." *Bulletin of the Council for Research in Music Education Bulletin* 33 (Summer 1973): 1-7.

Ulrich, Homer. "Convention Papers and Journal Articles." In *A Centennial History of the Music Teachers National Association*. Cincinnati, OH: Music Teachers National Association, Inc., 1976.

Van Camp, Leonard. "The Rise of American Choral Music and the A Cappella 'Bandwagon.'" *Music Educators Journal* 67 (November 1980): 36-40.

Warner, Roger W. "CM Reflections of a Band Director." *The Quarterly* 1 (Autumn 1990): 45-50.

Warren, Fred Anthony. "A History of the *Journal of Research in Music Education*, 1953-1965." *Journal of Research in Music Education* 32 (Winter 1984): 223-232.

Washburn, Robert. "Reflections on the MENC-CMP." *The Quarterly* 1 (Autumn 1990): 64-66.

Webster, Peter R. "The Ivory Tower, the Trenches, and the Gap Which Separates." *Contributions to Music Education* 7 (1979): 68-73.

Weigand, Joseph J. "Music in the Junior High School, 1900-1957." *Journal of Research in Music Education* 9 (Spring 1961): 55-62.

Weimer, George W. "Doctoral Dissertation Research in Music Education, 1963-1978: A Quantitative Analysis." *The Bulletin of Historical Research in Music Education* 7 (July 1986): 55-71.

Werner, Robert J. "A Case History of One Foundation's Philanthropy." *The Quarterly* (1 Autumn 1990): 5-9.

White, J. Perry. "Significant Developments in Choral Music Education in Higher Education Between 1950-1980." *Journal of Research in Music Education* 30 (Summer 1982): 121-128.

White, J. Perry, and George N. Heller. "Entertainment, Enlightenment, and Service: A History and Description of Choral Music in Higher Education." *College Music Symposium* 23 (Fall 1983): 10-20.

Whitehill, Charles D. "Sociological Conditions Which Contributed to the Growth of the School Band Movement in the United States." *Journal of Research in Music Education* 17 (Summer 1969): 179-192.

Willoughby, David. "Comprehensive Musicianship." *The Quarterly* 1 (Autumn 1990): 39-44.

Wilson, Bruce D., and Charles L. Gary. "The Sesquicentennial." [Special Issue] *Music Educators Journal* 74 (February 1988).

Woodbridge, William C. "Music as a Branch of Instruction in Common Schools." *American Journal of Education* (1830): 213-222.

Yarbrough, Cornelia. "A Content Analysis of the *Journal of Research in Music Education*." *Journal of Research in Music Education* 32 (Winter 1984): 213-222.

Yoder, Paul. "The Early History of the American Bandmasters Association, Part I." *The Journal of Band Research* 1 (Autumn 1964): 1-10; Part II *The Journal of Band Research* 1 (Winter 1965): 1-5; Part III *The Journal of Band Research 2 (Spring 1966): 4-8; Part IV, The Journal of Band Research* 3 (Autumn 1966): 39-44.

Young, Amanda, "Oral History—A Popular Research Technique That Can Work in Music Classes." *Music Educators Journal* 67 (November 1980): 52-55.

Zinar, Ruth. "Highlights of Thought on Music Education Through the Centuries." *The American Music Teacher* 32 (February-March 1983): 32-38; *The American Music Teacher* 33 (November-December 1983): 44; *The American Music Teacher* 33 (January 1984): 44; *The American Music Teacher* 33 (February-March 1984): 44; *The American Music Teacher* 33 (April-May 1984): 18.

Zorn, Jay. "The Changing Role of Instrumental Music." *Music Educators Journal* 76 (November 1989): 21-24.

Reviews

Bergee, Martin J. Review of *The Modern Researcher*, 4th ed., by Jacques Barzun and Henry F. Graff. In *The Bulletin of Historical Research in Music Education* 7 (July 1986): 75-77.

_____. Review of *The New Harvard Dictionary of Music*, edited by Don Michael Randel. In *The Bulletin of Historical Research in Music Education* 8 (January 1987): 55-57.

Berry, Lemuel, Jr. Review of "A Historical Survey of the Development of the Black Baptist Church in the United States and a Study of Performance Practices Associated with Dr. Watts' Hymn Singing: A Source Book for Teachers" (Ed.D. diss., Washington University, 1979), by Curtis Daniel Duncan. In *Bulletin of the Council for Research in Music Education* 66-67 (Spring-Summer 1981): 169-171.

Britton, Allen P. Review of *The New Grove Dictionary of American Music*, 4 vols., edited by H. Wiley Hitchcock and Stanley Sadie. In *American Music* 5 (Summer 1987): 194-203.

Carson, Sandra Cornell. Review of *The Music of Black Americans: A History*, 2nd ed., by Eileen Southern. In *The Bulletin of Historical Research in Music Education* 5 (January 1984): 22-23.

Cipolla, Frank J. Review of "Union Bands of the Civil War (1862-1865): Instrumentation and Score Analysis" (Ph.D. diss., Louisiana State University, 1973), by William Bufkin. In *Bulletin of the Council for Research in Music Education* 68 (Fall 1981): 67-68.

Coffman, Don D. Review of *A Pictorial History of Civil War Era Music Instruments and Military Bands*, by Robert Garfalo and Mark Elrod. In *The Bulletin of Historical Research in Music Education* 7 (July 1986): 78-79.

Cohen, Nicki S. Review of *Music in American Higher Education: An Annotated Bibliography*. Bibliographies in American Music, No. 10., by Edward Brookhart. In *The Bulletin of Historical Research in Music Education* 10 (July 1989): 111-113.

Darrow, Alice-Ann. Review of *Contemporary Music Education*, 2nd ed., by Michael L. Mark. In *The Bulletin of Historical Research in Music Education* 7 (July 1986): 73-75.

Farlow, Betsy C. Review of "A Brief History of White Southern Gospel Music and a Study of Selected Amateur Family Gospel" (Ph.D. diss., New York University, 1977), by Stanley H. Brobston. In *Bulletin of the Council for Research in Music Education* 69 (Winter 1982): 29-32.

Fisher, Robert E. Review of *Music in the New World*, by Charles Hamm. In *The Bulletin of Historical Research in Music Education* 5 (January 1984): 21-22.

_____. Review of *The New Oxford Companion to Music*, 2 vols., Denis Arnold, ed. In *The Bulletin of Historical Research in Music Education* 6 (January 1985): 35-36.

Gilbert, Janet Perkins. Review of *A Cross-Section of Research in Music Education*, by Stephen H. Barnes. In *The Bulletin of Historical Research Music Education* 3 (July 1982): 103-104

Grashel, John W. Review of *Foundations of Music Education*, by Harold F. Abeles, Charles R. Hoffer, and Robert H. Klotman. In *The Bulletin of Historical Research in Music Education* 6 (July 1985): 81-82.

_____. Review of *The Billboard Book of Top 40 Hits: 1955 to Present*, by Joel Whitburn. In *The Bulletin of Historical Research in Music Education* 6 (January 1985): 36-37.

Haack, Paul A. Review of *A History of Music in American Life*. Volume II: *The Gilded Years, 1865-1920*, by Ronald L. Davis. In *The Bulletin of Historical Research in Music Education* 2 (January 1981): 10-11.

Harris, Jean Noton. Review of "The Emergence of the Concept of General Music as Reflected in Basal Textbooks: 1900-1980" (D.M.A. diss., The Catholic University of America, 1985), by Florence Growman. In *Bulletin of the Council for Research in Music Education* 94 (Fall 1987): 56-59.

Heller, George N. Review of *American Popular Stage Music: 1860 1880*, by Dean L. Root. In *The Bulletin of Historical Research in Music Education* 3 (January 1982): 19-20.

_____. Review of *A Guide to Research in Music Education*, 2nd ed., by Roger P. Phelps. In *The Bulletin of Historical Research in Music Education* 2 (January 1981): 11-12.

_____. Review of *Hidden History: Exploring Our Secret Past*, by Daniel J. Boorstin. In *The Bulletin of Historical Research in Music Education* 11 (January 1990): 55-58.

_____. Review of *A History of Music Education in the United States*, by James A. Keene. In *Music Educators Journal* 69 (October 1982): 101-104.

_____. Review of *The Musical Imperative*, by Simon V. Anderson. In *The Bulletin of Historical Research in Music Education* 5 (July 1984): 61-62.

_____. Review of *Research in Music Education: An Introduction to Systematic Inquiry*, by Edward L. Rainbow and Hildegard C. Froelich. In *The Bulletin of Historical Research in Music Education* 9 (July 1988): 131-132.

_____. Review of *Since Socrates: Studies in the History of Western Education*, by Henry J. Perkinson. In *The Bulletin of Historical Research in Music Education* 1 (July 1980): 17.

_____. Review of *Source Readings in Music Education History*, by Michael L. Mark. In *The Bulletin of Historical Research in Music Education* 4 (July 1983): 39-40.

_____. Review of *Words on Music: From Addison to Barzun*, ed. by Jack Sullivan. *Bulletin of the Council for Research in Music Education* 110 (Fall 1991): 97-101.

Humphreys, Jere T. Review of *American Education: The Metropolitan Experience* by Lawrence A. Cremin. In *The Bulletin of Historical Research in Music Education* 12 (January 1991): 67-71.

_____. Review of "The Band Business in the United States Between the Civil War and the Great Depression" (Ph.D. diss., Weslayan University, 1987), by Christine Condaris. In *Bulletin of the Council for Research in Music Education* 104 (Spring 1990): 54-58.

_____. Review of *Hierarchy, History, and Human Nature: The Social Origins of Historical Consciousness*, by Donald E. Brown. In *The Bulletin of Historical Research in Music Education* 11 (January 1990): 48-54.

John, Robert W. Review of "The Music Educators National Conference Student Member Organization: Its History, a Critical Review of Current Programs Listed in the 1977 Handbook, and Future Professional Development" (Ph.D. diss., University of Oklahoma, 1979), by Leonard Lowell Lehman. In *Bulletin of the Council for Research in Music Education* 71 (Summer 1982): 81-84.

Kelley Steven N. Review of *Horatio Parker, 1863-1919: His Life, Music, and Ideas*. In *The Bulletin of Historical Research in Music Education* 12 (January 1991): 72-74.

May, William V. Review of *Education in a Free Society: An AMerican History*, by S. Alexander Rippa. *The Bulletin of Historical Research in Music Education* 2 (January 1981): 12.

Miller, Samuel D. Review of "The Instructional Philosophies Reflected in the Elementary Series Published by Silver Burdett Company, 1885-1975" (Ed.D. diss., University of Illinois, 1984), by Jean Noton Harris. *Bulletin of the Council for Research in Music Education* 94 (Fall 1987): 48-52.

O'Connor, Mary Alice. Review of "Music Education in the Catholic Schools: A Content Analysis of *Musart, Caecilia (Sacred Music)*, and the *Catholic School Journal (Momentum)* (1954-1975)" (Ph.D. diss., The Florida State University, 1978), by Phyllis E. Nutting. *Bulletin of the Council for Research in Music Education* 70 (Spring 1982): 64-69.

Parker, Harlan D. Review of *Discoursing Sweet Music: Brass Bands and Community Life in Turn-of-the-Century Pennsylvania*, by Kenneth Kreitner. In *The Bulletin of Historical Research in Music Education* 11 (July 1990): 135-137.

Rives, James A. Review of *Listening to History: The Authenticity of Oral Evidence*, by Trevor Lummis. In *The Bulletin of Historical Research in Music Education* 10 (July 1989): 113-117.

Scholten, James W. Review of *The New Grove Dictionary of American Music*, edited by H. Wiley Hitchcock and Stanley Sadie. *The Bulletin of Historical Research in Music Education* 9 (January 1988): 61-67.

Scott, Carol Rogel. Review of "Preschool Music Education and Research on the Musical Development of Preschool Children: 1900 to 1980" (Ph.D. diss., The University of Michigan, 1981), by Barbara Jo Alvarez. *Bulletin of the Council for Research in Music Education* 87 (Spring 1986): 57-61.

Sharp, Timothy W. Review of "An Index of Choral Music Performed During National Conventions of the American Choral Directors Association (1960-1987)" (Ph.D. diss., The Florida State University, 1988), by William Darryl Jones. In *Bulletin of the Council for Research in Music Education* 104 (Spring 1990): 76-80.

Sink, Patricia E. Review of *A Guide to Historical Methods*, by Robert J. Shafer. *The Bulletin of Historical Research in Music Education* 4 (January 1983): 16-17.

———. Review of *Yesterdays: Popular Songs in America*, by Charles Hamm. *The Bulletin of Historical Research in Music Education* 1 (July 1980): 18-19.

Standifer, James A. Review of "The Life Story of the Blues Musician: An Analysis of the Tradition of Oral Self-Portrayal" (Ph.D. diss., Indiana University, 1977), by Barry Lee Pearson. *Bulletin of the Council for Research in Music Education* 69 (Winter 1982): 36-39.

Steel, David Warren. Review of "Analysis of the Music Curriculum of Sacred Harp (American Tune-Book, 1971 Edition) and Its Continuing Traditions" (Ed.D. diss., University of Alabama, 1985), by Mai Hogan Kelton. In *Bulletin of the Council for Research in Music Education* 103 (Winter 1990): 39-43.

Tulley, Robert J. Review of "Multicultural Music Education: An Analysis of Afro-American and Native American Folk Songs in Selected Elementary Music Textbooks of the Periods 1928-1955 and 1965-1975" (Ph.D. diss., The University of Michigan, 1977), by Marvelene Clarissa Moore. *Bulletin of the Council for Research in Music Education* 62 (Spring 1980): 59-61

Velásquez, Vivian. Review of *History and Computing II*, Stefan Fogelvik and Charles Harvey, eds. In *The Bulletin of Historical Research in Music Education* 12 (January 1991): 63-66.

Dissertations

Alper, Clifford D. "The Influence of Froebel's Mother-Play and Nursery Songs on Kindergarten Song Books, 1887-1918." Ph.D. diss., University of Maryland, 1972.

Alvarez, Barbara J. "Preschool Music Education and Research on the Musical Development of Preschool Children: 1900 to 1980." Ph.D. diss., The University of Michigan, 1981.

Austin, Henry R. "History of Broadcasting at the National Music Camp, Interlochen, Michigan." Ed.D. diss., The University of Michigan, 1959.

Baird, Frank W. "A History and Annotated Bibliography of Tutors for Trumpet and Cornet." Ph.D. diss., The University of Michigan, 1983.

Bauer, David A. "The Influence of the ACDA upon Choral Music in the Decade of the 1970s." Ed.D. diss., Arizona State University, 1985.

Bean, Shirley A. "*The Missouri Harmony*, 1820-1858: The Refinement of a Southern Tunebook." D.M.A. diss., University of Missouri, Kansas City, 1973.

Becknell, Arthur F. "A History of the Development of Dalcroze Eurythmics in the United States and Its Influence on the Public School Music Program." Ed.D. diss., The University of Michigan, 1970.

Bellingham, Bruce A. "The Bicinium in the Lutheran Latin Schools During the Reformation Period." Ph.D. diss., University of Toronto, 1971.

Benson, Norman A. "The Itinerant Dancing and Music Masters of Eighteenth Century America." Ph.D. diss., University of Minnesota, 1963.

Blum, Beula B. "Solmization in Nineteenth-Century American Sight-Singing Instruction." Ed.D. diss., The University of Michigan, 1968.

Bostrum, Marvin J. "Keyboard Instruction Books of the Eighteenth Century." Ph.D. diss., The University of Michigan, 1961.

Boxberger, Ruth. "A Historical Study of the National Association for Music Therapy." Ph.D. diss., The University of Kansas, 1963.

Branch, London G. "Jazz Education in Predominantly Black Colleges." Ph.D. diss., Southern Illinois University, 1976.

Britton, Allen P. "Theoretical Introductions in American Tune-Books to 1800." Ph.D. diss., The University of Michigan, 1950.

Brooke, Margaret B. "Women: Pedagogues, Performers, and Composers as Presented by *The Etude* Magazine During the Years of Women's Suffrage, 1897-1920." D.M.A. diss., University of Iowa, 1987.

Burdett, Noreen D. "The High School Music Contest Movement in the United States." Mus.A.D. diss., Columbia University, 1954.

Butler, David M. "An Historical Investigation and Bibliography of Nineteenth-Century Music Psychology Literature." Ph.D. diss., The Ohio State University, 1973.

Bynum, Alton C. "Music Programs and Practices of the Christian and Missionary Alliance." Ed.D. diss., New Orleans Baptist Theological Seminary, 1975.

Carpenter, Thomas H. "An Analysis of Past, Present, and Potential Uses of Instructional Television in the Teaching of Music." D.M.A. diss., Boston University, 1965.

Chapman, Charles W. "A Survey of Elementary Concepts of Voice Production Reflected in American Monographs on Vocal Pedagogy from 1875 to 1920." Ph.D. diss., University of Texas, 1971.

Cheek, Curtis L. "The Singing School and Shaped-Note Tradition: Residuals in Twentieth-Century American Hymnody." D.M.A. diss., University of Southern California, 1968.

Cleave, Howard E. "The Organization and Development of the Elementary School Recreational Band." Ed.D. diss., Columbia University, 1968.

Collins, Charlotte A. "Public School Music Certification in Historical Perspective." Ed.D. diss., The University of Michigan, 1970.

Colman, Barry H. "Origins of American Wind Music and General Instrumental Tutors." D.A. diss., University of Northern Colorado, 1985.

Condaris, Christine. "The Band Business in the United States Between the Civil War and the Great Depression." Ph.D. diss., Wesleyan University, 1986.

Cook, Bruce F. "Twenty-Five Years of Music Competition under University Interscholastic League Administration." D.M.A. diss., University of Texas, 1975.

Copenhaver, Harold L. "An Historical Investigation of Music Education in the United States Air Force." Ed.D. diss., The American University, 1961.

Cross, Virginia A. "The Development of Sunday School Hymnody in the United States of America, 1816-1869." D.M.A. diss., New Orleans Baptist Theological Seminary, 1985.

Darrow, Gerald F. "The Nature of Choral Training as Revealed Through Analysis of Thirty-Three Years of Published Writings." Mus.Ed.D. diss, Indiana University, 1965.

Davis, Alan L. "A History of the American Bandmasters Association." D.M.A. diss., Arizona State University, 1987.

Davison, Sr. Mary Veronica. "American Music Periodicals, 1853-1899." Ph.D. diss., University of Minnesota, 1973.

DeFries, Stanley L. "An Analysis of Preference Patterns in Choral Programs in the United States of America, 1900-1958." Ph.D. diss., Indiana University, 1966.

DeJournett, Ned R. "The History and Development of the American Choral Directors Association, 1957-1970." Ph.D. diss., The Florida State University, 1970.

Diaz, Margaret C. "An Analysis of the Elementary School Music Series Published in the United States from 1926 to 1976." Ed.D. diss., University of Illinois, 1980.

Duke, John R. "Teaching Musical Improvisation: A Study of Eighteenth and Twentieth Century Methods." George Peabody College for Teachers, 1972.

Dunham, Richard L. "Music Appreciation in the Public Schools of the United States, 1897-1930." Ph.D. diss., The University of Michigan, 1961.

Ellis, Howard E. "The Influence of Pestalozzianism on Instruction in Music." Ph.D. diss., The University of Michigan, 1957.

Estes, William P. "Change in Status of Music Education Between 1955-56 and 1961-62 in Public School Systems of Selected Cities Between 50,000 and 100,000 Population." Ed.D. diss., University of Illinois, 1964.

Fain, Samuel S. "The Community Symphony Orchestra in the United States, 1750 to 1955." D.M.A. diss., University of Southern California, 1956.

Farley, Charles R. "Contrasts in Vocal Pedagogy: 1940 and 1970." D.Mus.Ed., The University of Oklahoma, 1971.

Faulkner, Maurice E. "The Roots of Music Education in American Colleges and Universities." Ph.D. diss., Stanford University, 1956.

FitzPatrick, Edward J. "The Music Conservatory in America." Mus.A.D., Boston University, 1963.

Forbis, Wesley L. "The Galin-Paris-Chevé Method of Rhythmic Instruction: A History." Ph.D. diss., George Peabody College for Teachers, 1970.

Fouts, Gordon E. "Music Instruction in America to Around 1830 as Suggested by the Hartzler Collection of Early Protestant American Tune Books." Ph.D. diss., The University of Iowa, 1968.

Fritts, C. Nelson. "The Historic Development of the Concept of Comprehensive Musicianship in School Bands." D.M.A. diss., The Catholic University of America, 1991.

Fullbright, Wilbur D. "The History and Development of the Master's Degree in Music in the United States." Ph.D. diss., Boston University, 1960.

Gegermeier, Sr. Mary Joyce. "The Role of Music in the Junior College." Ph.D. diss., The University of Michigan, 1967.

Goodman, A. Harold. "Development of the Symphony Orchestra in Higher Education." Ed.D. diss., University of Southern California, 1960.

Gray, Sharon L. "History of the National Catholic Music Educators' Association, 1942-1976." D.M.E. diss., University of Cincinnati, 1988.

Grimes, Calvin B. "American Musical Periodicals, 1819-1852: Music Theory and Musical Thought in the United States." Ph.D. diss., The University of Iowa, 1974.

Grover, Paul B. "The History of String Class Instruction in American Schools and Its Relationship to School Orchestras." Ed.D. diss., University of Illinois, 1960.

Growman, Florence. "The Emergence of the Concept of General Music as Reflected in Basal Textbooks: 1900-1980." D.M.A. diss., The Catholic University of America, 1985.

Hall, Paul M. "The *Musical Million*: A Study and Analysis of the Periodical Promoting Music Reading Through Shape-Notes in North America from 1870 to 1914." D.M.A. diss., The Catholic University of America, 1970.

Halseth, Robert E. P. "The Impact of the College Band Directors National Association on Wind Band Repertoire." D.A. diss., University of Northern Colorado, 1987.

Hammett, Thomas F. "*The Choral Journal*: An Annotated Index to Volumes 19-24 and a Comparison of Subject Material Published in Volumes 1-18 and 19-24." Ed.D. diss., The Florida State University, 1985.

Harris, Jean N. "Philosophies Reflected in the Elementary Music Series Published by Silver Burdett Company, 1885-1975." Ed.D. diss., University of Illinois, 1985.

Harris, John M. "The Pedagogical Development of College Harmony Textbooks in the United States." D.M.A. diss., The University of Texas, 1969.

Haynie, Jerry T. "The Changing Role of the Band in American Colleges and Universities, 1900-1968." Ph.D. diss., George Peabody College for Teachers, 1971.

Henderson, Robert V. "Solmization Syllables in Music Theory, 1100 to 1600." Ph.D. diss., Columbia University, 1969.

Herfort, David V. "A History of the National Association of Jazz Educators and a Description of Its Role in American Music Education, 1968-1978." Ed.D. diss., University of Houston, 1979.

Hill, Melvin S. "A History of Music Education in Seventh-Day Adventist Western Colleges." D.Mus.A. diss., University of Southern California, 1959.

Himrod, Gail P. "The Music Education Movement in the United States, 1830-1860." Ph.D. diss., Boston University, 1989.

Holz, Emil A. "The National School Band Tournament and Its Bands." Ph.D. diss., The University of Michigan, 1960.

Hooper, Maureen D. "Major Concerns of Music Education: Content Analysis of the *Music Educators Journal*, 1957-1967." Ed.D. diss., University of Southern California, 1969.

Hooper, William L. "The Master's Degree in Church Music in Protestant Theological Seminaries of the United States." Ph.D. diss., George Peabody College for Teachers, 1966.

Houlihan, James E. "The Music Educators National Conference in American Education." Ph.D. diss., Boston University, 1961.

Hounchell, Robert F. "A Study of Creativity and Music Reading as Objectives of Music Education as Contained in Statements in the *Music Educators Journal* from 1914 to 1970." Ph.D. diss., Indiana University, 1985.

Huizenga, Gertrude A. "An Index of *The National Association of Teachers of Singing Bulletin*, 1945-1956." Ph.D. diss., Michigan State University

Hunt, Leslie J. "An Analysis of College Music Education Positions in the Academic Labor Market from 1973-1981." D.Mus.Ed. diss., Indiana University, 1983.

Hurst, Olive W. "A Comparative Historical Analysis of the Relationship of Public School Music to Education and to Music." Ph.D. diss., The Ohio State University, 1951.

Ingle, Gary L. "An Annotated Bibliography of Books, Articles, Theses, and Dissertations Related to the Training of Choral Ensembles, 1959-1984." D.M.A. diss., Southern Baptist Theological Seminary, 1988.

Jacoby, Hugh W. "Selected American Composers Affiliated with American Colleges and Universities: Biographical Sketches, Their Productively, Professional Status, Performance of Works and Attitudes Toward University Patronage." Ed.D. diss., Washington University, 1974.

James, Janice L. "The Music of Afro-Americans in Elementary Music Series Books: An Investigation of Changing Textbook Content, 1864-1970." Ph.D. diss., University of Southern Mississippi, 1976.

James, Richard L. "A Survey of Teacher Training Programs in Music from the Early Musical Convention to the Introduction of Four-Year Degree Curricula." Ed.D. diss, University of Maryland, 1968.

Jennings, Robert L. "A Study of the Historical Development of Choral Ensembles in Selected Lutheran Liberal Arts Colleges in the United States." Ph.D. diss., Michigan State University, 1969.

John, Robert W. "A History of School Vocal Instruction Books in the United States." Mus.Ed.D. diss., Indiana University, 1953.

Johnson. Peter R. "MENC as Arbiter of Taste for Secondary School Chorus." Ph.D. diss., The University of Michigan, 1969.

Jones, Walter R. "An Analysis of Public School Music Textbooks Before 1900." Ed.D. diss., University of Pittsburgh, 1954.

Jones, William D. "An Index of Choral Music Performed During National Conventions of the American Choral Directors Association (1960-1987)." Ph.D. diss., The Florida State University, 1988.

Jones, William M. "A Study of Values in Music Education, 1950-1970." Ed.D. diss., University of the Pacific, 1973.

Jordan, William S. "Time, Space, and Music: Prolegomena to the History of Musical Theory." Ph.D. diss., The Florida State University, 1976.

Karjala, H. Eugene. "A Critical Analysis of *School Music Magazine* 1900-1936." Ph.D. diss., University of Minnesota, 1973.

Kauffman, Harry M. "A History of the Music Educators National Conference." Ph.D. diss., George Peabody College for Teachers, 1942.

Kaufman, Lee J. "A Historical Study of Seven-Character Shaped Note Music Notation." Ed.D. diss., University of Virginia, 1970.

Kegerreis, Richard I. "History of the High School a Cappella Choir." Ph.D. diss., The University of Michigan, 1966.

Kendall, Susan E. "The Significance of Innovators Ideas and Enduring Values in Music Education." Ph.D. diss., University of York [UK], 1989.

Kennedy, Arthur W. "The Doctoral Degree in Music in Universities and Colleges of the United States." Ph.D. diss., Northwestern University, 1955.

Kennedy, Thomas F. "Jesuits and Music: The European Tradition, 1547-1622." Ph.D. diss., University of California, Santa Barbara, 1982.

Kent, Richard L. "Music in Democratic Education: An Evaluation of Publications of Committees, Councils, and Commissions of the National Education Association of the United States." Mus.A.D. Diss., Boston University, 1961.

Kersten, Fred G. "An Analysis of Music Education Methods and Materials for the Visually Impaired Synthesized from Documents Written Between 1891 and 1978." Ed.D. diss., Pennsylvania State University, 1979.

Kidd, Robert W. "The Music Educators National Conference in the 1960s: An Analysis of Curricular Philosophy." Mus.A.D. diss., Boston University, 1984.

Kite, Thomas S. "The Organization of American Kodály Educators: Its History and Impact on American Music Education." Ed.D. diss., University of Houston, 1985.

Koch, Franklin W. "The History and Promotional Activities of the National Bureau for the Advancement of Music." Ph.D. diss., The University of Michigan, 1973.

Koza, Julia Eklund. "Music and References to Music in 'Godey's Lady's Book,' 1830-77." Ph.D. diss., University of Minnesota, 1988.

Kraft, Ivor. "Education for Idiots: Caring for the Mentally Retarded in Nineteenth-Century America." Ph.D. diss., Johns Hopkins University, 1962.

Lake, Carlton. "A Survey of the Music and Music Festivals of the Welsh." D.Mus. diss., Philadelphia Conservatory of Music, 1960.

Landon, Esther. "Seventeenth- and Eighteenth-Century English and Colonial American Music Texts: An Analysis of Instructional Content." Ph.D. diss., University of California, Los Angeles, 1977.

Laramore, Douglas L. "A History of the National Trumpet Symposium, 1968-1973, Including a Study of Selected Pedagogical Lectures." D.M.A. diss., The University of Oklahoma, 1990.

Lasko, Richard. "A History of the College Band Directors National Association." Ed.D. diss., University of Cincinnati, 1971.

Laycock, Harold R. "A History of Music in the Academies of the Latter-Day Saints Church, 1876-1926." D.Mus.A. diss., University of Southern California, 1961.

Lebow, Marcia W. "A Systematic Examination of the *Journal of Music and Art*." Ph.D. diss., The University of Michigan, 1969.

Lee, Cecil L. "Developing Patterns of the Undergraduate Music Education Curriculum in the United States." Ph.D. diss., Brigham Young University, 1965.

Lehman, Leonard L. "The Music Educators National Conference Student Member Organization: Its History, A Critical Review of Current Programs Recommended in the 1977 *Handbook*, and Recommendations for future Pre-Professional Development." Ph.D. diss., The University of Oklahoma, 1979.

Lindsley, Charles E. "Early Nineteenth-Century American Collections of Sacred Choral Music, 1800-1810." Ph.D. diss., The University of Iowa, 1968.

Loessel, Earl O. "The Use of Character Notes and Other Unorthodox Notations in Teaching the Reading of Music in Northern United States During the Nineteenth Century." Ph.D. diss., The University of Michigan, 1959.

Mack, Joan M. "The Transition Period in Violoncello Pedagogy as Manifested in Violoncello Methods from 1830 to 1910." A.Mus.D. diss., The University of Rochester, 1962.

Mathis, William E. "The Development of Practices Involving Simple Instruments in Elementary Music Programs, 1900-1960." Ph.D. diss., The University of Michigan, 1969.

Mathison, Curtis J. "The Teaching of the Theory of Music in American High Schools from 1900 to 1930." Ed.D. diss., The University of Michigan, 1972.

Maust, Earl M. "The History and Development of Music in Mennonite-Controlled Liberal Arts Colleges in the United States." Ed.D. diss., George Peabody College for Teachers, 1968.

McCann, John L. "A History of Trumpet and Cornet Pedagogy in the United States, 1840-1942." D.M. diss., Northwestern University, 1989.

McCarrell, Lamar K. "A Historical Review of the College Band Movement from 1875 to 1969." Ph.D. diss., The Florida State University, 1971.

Messer, Susan K. "The Southern Baptist Children's Choir Curricula from 1941 Through 1985 and Influences of Major Music Education Trends Upon the Curricula." Ph.D. diss., Louisiana State University, 1988.

Meyer, Janet L. "Change in Status of Music Education Between 1955 and 1961 in Public Schools of Selected Cities Between 100,000 and 200,000 Population." Ed.D. diss., University of Illinois, 1963.

Miller, Thomas W. "The Influence of Progressivism on Music Education, 1917-1947." Mus.A.D. diss., Boston University, 1964.

Molnar, John W. "The History of the Music Educators National Conference." Ed.D. diss., University of Cincinnati, 1948.

Monsour, Sally A. "The Establishment and Early Development of Beginning Piano Classes in the Public Schools, 1915-1930." Ed.D. diss., The University of Michigan, 1960.

Moore, George E. "An Appraisal of Seven Harmony Textbooks Used in American Institutions of Higher Learning at the Undergraduate Level During the 1955-56 School Year." Ed.D. diss., Columbia University, 1959.

Moore, James E. "The National School Band Contests from 1926-1931." Ph.D. diss., The University of Michigan, 1968.

Morlan, Gene. "Programs of Action for State Music Educators Associations." Ed.D. diss., George Peabody College for Teachers, 1966.

Mountney, Virginia R. "The History of the Bachelor's Degree in the Field of Music in the United States." Mus.A.D. diss., Boston University, 1961.

Neil R. J. "The Development of the Competition-Festival in Music Education." Ph.D. diss., George Peabody College for Teachers, 1944.

Neuchterlein, Herbert E. "The Sixteenth-Century Schulkantorei and Its Participation in the Lutheran Service." Ph.D. diss., The University of Michigan, 1969.

Neumeyer, Carl Melvin. "A History of the National Association of Schools of Music." Mus.Ed.D. diss., Indiana University, 1954.

Neve, Paul E. "The Contribution of the Lutheran College Choirs to Music in America." S.M.D. diss., Union Theological Seminary, 1967.

Norman, John L. "A Historical Study of the Changes in Attitudes Toward the Teaching of Piano Technique from 1800 to the Present." Ph.D. diss., Michigan State University, 1969.

Nutting, Phyllis E. "Music Education in the Catholic Schools: A Content Analysis of *Musart, Caecilia (Sacred Music)*, and *The Catholic School Journal (Momentum)* (1954-1975)." Ph.D. diss., The Florida State University, 1978.

Osterby, Patricia M. "Orff Schulwerk in North America, 1955-69." Ed.D. diss., University of Illinois, 1988.

Oursler, Robert D. "The Effect of Pestalozzian Theory and Practice on Music Education in the United States Between 1850 and 1900." Ph.D. diss., Northwestern University, 1966.

Peabody, Ada I. "Music by Recognized Composers in Elementary School Music Textbooks Published in the United States, 1870 Through 1959." Ph.D. diss., Indiana University, 1963.

Pierce, Charles L. "A History of Music and of Music Education of the Seventh-Day Adventist Church." D.M.A. diss., The Catholic University of America, 1976.

Pinkston, Alfred A. "Lined Hymns, Spirituals, and the Associated Lifestyle of Rural Black People in the United States." Ph.D. diss., University of Miami, 1975.

Piper, Robert N. "An Evaluation of the ACDA *Choral Journal*." Ed.D. diss., University of Illinois, 1972.

Poff, David G. "Summer Schools of Music Sponsored by Publishing Companies, 1888-1920." Ph.D. diss., The University of Michigan, 1970.

Regier, Bernard W. "The Development of Choral Music in Higher Education." D.M.A. Diss., University of Southern California, 1963.

Rhoden, Jane O. "A History of Music Written for Pre-School Children." Ph.D. diss., The Florida State University, 1969.

Richards, William H. "Trends of Piano Class Instruction, 1815-1962." University of Missouri Kansas City, 1962.

Ricks, Barbara S. "Innovations in Undergraduate Music Education Curricula from 1968 Through 1973 in College and Universities Which Are Members of the National Association of Schools of Music." Ed.D. diss., The University of Mississippi, 1974.

Riley, Maurice W. "The Teaching of Bowed Instruments from 1511 to 1756." Ph.D. diss., The University of Michigan, 1954.

Ritsema, Robert A. "A History of the American String Teachers Association: The First Twenty-Five Years." Ed.D. diss., The University of Michigan, 1971.

Rivers, Travis S. "*The Etude* Magazine: A Mirror of the Genteel Tradition in American Music." Ph.D. diss, The University of Iowa, 1974.

Rogers, Samuel K. "The Social and Pedagogical Function of *The Worcester Collection*, *The Village Harmony*, and *The Easy Instructor* in the Early-American Singing School." Ph.D. diss., The Florida State University, 1969.

Sanders, Constance A. "A History of Radio in Music Education in the United States with Emphasis on the Activities of Music Educators and on Certain Radio Music Series Designed for Elementary and Secondary Use." D.M.E. diss., University of Cincinnati, 1990.

Savage, Edith J. "The Development of Instruction in Music Reading in Public Schools of the United States." Ed.D. diss, The University of Colorado, 1960.

Schoof, Jack E. "A Study of Didactic Attitudes on the Fine Arts in America as Expressed in Popular Magazines During the Period 1786-1800." Ph.D. diss., The Ohio State University, 1967.

Shaum, David W. "The Music Program in Catholic Colleges and Universities in the U.S." Ph.D. diss., The Catholic University of America, 1961.

Slaughter, Jay L. "The Role of Music in the Mormon Church, School, and Life." Ed.D. diss., Indiana University, 1964.

Smith, Lamar. "A Study of the Historical Development of Selected Black College and University Bands as a Curricular and Aesthetic Entity, 1867-1975." Ph.D. diss., Kansas State University, 1976.

Sollinger, Charles E. "The Music Men and the Professors: A History of String Class Methods in the United States, 1800-1911." Ed.D. diss., The University of Michigan, 1970.

Spell, Lota M. "Musical Education in North America During the Sixteenth and Seventeenth Centuries." Ph.D. diss., University of Texas, 1923.

Stabler, Dennis G. "A Content Analysis of the *Bulletin of the Council for Research in Music Education*, 1963-1985." Ed.D. diss., University of Illinois, 1986.

Stanislaw, Richard J. "Choral Performance Practice in the Four-Shape Literature of American Frontier Singing Schools." D.M.A. diss., University of Illinois, 1976.

Steele, Daniel L. "An Investigation into the Background and Implications of the Yale Seminar on Music Education." D.M.E. diss., University of Cincinnati, 1988.

Stone, Margaret L. "Kodály and Orff Music Teaching Techniques: History and Present Practice." Ph.D. diss., Kent State University, 1971.

Stroud, William P. "The Ravenscroft Psalter (1621): The Tunes, with a Background on Thomas Ravenscroft and Psalm Singing in His Time." D.Mus.A. diss., University of Southern California, 1959.

Sunderman, Lloyd F. "A History of Public School Music in the United States (1830-1890)." Ph.D. diss., University of Minnesota, 1939.

Super, Sr. Dolores. "Musical Performance in American Higher Education: 1850-1951." Ed.D. diss., The University of Michigan, 1970.

Taylor, Camille C. "The First Decade of the Black Music Caucus of the Music Educators National Conference." Ed.D. diss., Teachers College, Columbia University, 1984.

Taylor, William H. "The History and Development of Jazz Piano: A New Perspective for Educators." Ed.D. diss., University of Massachusetts, 1975.

Tellstrom, A. Theodore. "The Philosophical and Psychological Foundations of Music Education in the Nineteenth Century." Mus.A.D. diss., Boston University, 1957.

Texter, Merry E. "A Historical and Analytical Investigation of the Beginning Band Method Book." Ph.D. diss., The Ohio State University, 1975.

Thomas, Arnold R. "The Development of Male Glee Clubs in American Colleges and Universities." Ed.D. diss., Columbia University, 1962.

Topp, Gordon D. "Recorded Music Recommended for Teach Music Appreciation in Elementary Schools, 1912-1966." Ph.D. diss., The University of Michigan, 1967.

Van Camp, Leonard W. "The Development and Present Status of a Cappella Singing in United States Colleges and Universities." D.M.A. diss., University of Missouri, Kansas City, 1964.

Van Wright, Aaron. "Factors Relative to Job Selections in Music Faculties of the Original Negro Land-Grant Colleges since the 1954 Supreme Court Decision." Ed.D. diss., University of Oklahoma, 1965.

Warren, Fred A. "A History of the Music Education Research Council and the *Journal of Research in Music Education* of the Music Educators National Conference." Ed.D. diss., The University of Michigan, 1966.

Weimer, George W. "Trends in Topics, Methods of Research, and Statistical Techniques Employed in Dissertations Completed for Doctor's Degrees in Music Education, 1963-1978." Ed.D. diss., University of Illinois, 1980.

Wetzel, Richard D. "The Music of George Rapp's Harmony Society: 1805-1906." Ph.D. diss., University of Pittsburgh, 1970.

Whitinger, Julius E. "Hymnody of the Early American Indian Missions." Ph.D. diss., The Catholic University of America, 1971.

Wolverton, Byron A. "Keyboard Music and Musicians in the Colonies and United States of America Before 1830." Ph.D. diss., Indiana University, 1966.

Wooden, Ronald L. "Education Reform: Parallels in Music Education." Ph.D. diss., University of Utah, 1975.

Worthington, Richard A. "An Analysis of Doctoral Theses in Music Education, 1940-1954." Ed.D. diss., University of Illinois, 1956.

Wunderlich, Charles E. "A History and Bibliography of Early American Musical Periodicals, 1782-1852." Ph.D. diss., The University of Michigan, 1962.

Theses

Anderson, Raymond L. "A Comparative Survey of the Texts on Choral Conducting from 1800 to 1953." Master's thesis, Texas Christian University, 1953.

Barker, Edna. "Creative Musical Activity: Its History and Present Status in Education." Master's thesis, University of Washington, 1933.

Bennett, Barbara. "The History and Development of Class String Methodology in the United Sates." Master's thesis, Baylor University, 1967.

Bradley, Erelyne H. "Trends in Elementary School Music Since 1920." Master's thesis, Texas Christian University, 1954.

Breed, Victor T. "The Scholae Cantorum in the Early Middle Ages." Master's thesis, University of Arizona, 1930.

Brigham, Anna E. "A History of Music Education by Radio." Master's thesis, The University of Kansas, 1947.

Burgess, Eleanor Wood. "History of Children's Music in the Public School." Master's thesis, Ball State University, 1956.

Bushnell, Dorla P. "A Half Century of Elementary Music Education (from 1900 to 1950)." Master's thesis, Northwestern University, 1952.

Callahan, Maurice. "The History and Development of the Symphonic Band." Master's thesis, Colorado State College of Education, 1947.

Campbell, Pauline K. "Development in American Musical Education, 1914-1943." Master's thesis, Stanford University, 1947.

Cook, Wanda. "Methodology in Public School Music: A Survey of Changes in the Aims and Procedures of Music Teaching in the Public Schools During the Past One Hundred Years." Master's thesis, Michigan State University, 1939.

Corbin, Charles D. "Trends in Senior High School Music Education, 1900-1952." Master's thesis, University of Southern California, 1952.

Dean, Jerry M. "A History of Solmization and a Cooperative Study of American Pitch Verbalization Methods." Master's thesis, University of Texas, 1965.

Dickey, Frances M. "The Early History of Public School Music in the United States." Master's thesis, Teacher College, Columbia University, 1913.

Edwards, Ann M. "A History of Vocal Music in the Public Schools of the United States from 1830 to 1930." Master's thesis, Stanford University, 1947.

Elder, Frances R. "Historical Review and Critical Resume of Beginning String Class Materials, Methods, and Devices." Master's thesis, Texas Christian University, 1950.

Ewert, John L. "Music Education in Mennonite Academies." Master's thesis, Kansas State Teachers College, Emporia, 1951.

Fuhrman, William. "Public School Music in the United States, A History: Its Present Scope, A Brief Survey of Current Practices and Newer Tendencies." Master's thesis, Stanford University, 1933.

Garton, Jeanette. "History of Sight Singing and Its Use in the Modern School." Master's thesis, University of Denver, 1947.

Goldberg, Norman A. "History of the Band in the United States Since 1860." Master's thesis, Northwestern University, 1942.

Haid, Sr. Maris Stella. "The Organization and Influence of the National Catholic Music Educators Association." Master's thesis, The Ohio State University, 1947.

Hanner, Pat. "Solmization as a Teaching Device in Early American Music Education." Master's thesis, Hardin-Simmons University, 1967.

Halstead, Edwin E. "Music Appreciation in the Public Schools: Its History, Meaning, and Aim, and the Principles and Techniques Governing Its Development." Master's thesis, New York University, 1929

Henley, Glenice. "A Historical Survey of Music Appreciation in the Public Schools of the United States." Master"s thesis, University of Arizona, 1951.

Hoerr, Rosellen. "Trends in Teaching Music Fundamentals as Revealed Through Periodical Literature and Bulletins from 1900 to 1950." Master's thesis, Illinois State University, 1954.

Jones, Rachel. "A History of Public School Music in America." Master's thesis, New York University, 1928.

Jones, Sarah Ellen. "Music Appreciation in America: Its History and Typical Units of Study." Master's thesis, Northwestern University, 1946.

Kamp, Mary Z. "A Study of the Trends in the History of Public School Music." Master's thesis, University of Arizona, 1947.

Kramer, Carlisle H. "History of Public Secondary School Instrumental Music Methods of Class Instruction in the United States." Master's thesis, Stanford University, 1942.

Lamkin, Joe M. "Early Band Programs in the Schools of the Midwest and Southwest." Master's thesis, Baylor University, 1969.

Lawrence, Clara. "History of the Development of Public School Music Methods in America." Master's thesis, Northwestern University, 1934.

Maladey, Elizabeth. "Historical Survey of Theories and Methods Used by Teachers of Singing." Master's thesis, Duquesne University, 1940.

McKoown, Catherine. "Elementary School Music Education in the United States from 1800-1900." Master's thesis, Northwestern University, 1951.

Mikita, Andrew. "A Critical History of School Music Contests and Festivals in the United States." Master's thesis, University of Illinois, 1941.

Monroe, Samuel F. "The Development of Instrumental Music in the Public Schools of the United States." Master's thesis, New York University, 1930.

Mook, Kenneth C. "An Analytical and Historical Study of Three Specified Schools of Music." Master's thesis, Northwestern University, 1929.

Moore, Katrina Lee. "The History of the Development of Public School Music in Taylor County, Texas." Master's thesis, North Texas State Teachers College, 1943.

Murphy, Charles R. "History of the Piano Class in the United States–An Approach to Piano Playing for Class Instruction." Master's thesis, Boston University, 1950.

Petry, Delano Lee. "A History of the String Class and Orchestra in the Public Schools of the United States." Master's thesis, The University of Michigan, 1955.

Pfeil, William V. "The Competition Festival Since 1945." Master's thesis, Texas Christian University, 1952.

Reiss, Muriel. "Development of Music Education in the United States." Master's thesis, New England Conservatory of Music, 1949.

Rice, Karen W. "Bibliography of Music Research in the Southern Division, Music Educators National Conference, 1913-1968." Master's thesis, University of Georgia, 1968.

Ross, Carolyn W. "History of Music Education in the United States Since 1900." Master's thesis, The Catholic University of America, 1968.

Spell, Lota M. "A History of Musical Education in the United States." Master's thesis, University of Texas, 1919.

Swift, Hargrave. "A Historical Study of the Development of the High School Band." Master's thesis, University of Southern California, 1939.

Swiney, James M. "The Effect of Musical Education on Music Trends in the United States, 1940-1960." Master's thesis, American University, 1962.

White, Bernice. "Music Dictation: An Overview of the Subject, Including Its History, Something of Its Status in Music Curricula, A Comparison of Scholastic Standards, Conclusions, and Suggestions." Master's thesis, New York University, 1931.

Wolverton, Josephine. "Eighteenth-Century Music Teaching in America." Master's thesis, Northwestern University, 1937.

Zearfoss, Ruth. "The History of Music Education in the United States, 1838-1900." Master's thesis, Case Western Reserve University, 1956.